GOD'S HOTEL
Godspotting in all directions

David Wood

Egremont Today

1

GOD'S HOTEL

is

published by

E2D
Egremont Today
Waverley
Greendykes
Egremont
Cumbria CA22 2IS

www.egremont-today.com

Any profits will go to the Copeland Rungwe Tanzania Link (this exchange has for decades, provided an enormous variety of practical and technical skills with gifts of equipment. And most important perhaps many celebrations of friendships through schools exchanges and beyond).

CONTENTS

Preface

Egremont Today

'Godspotting', the Godspot, owes its existence to Egremont Today, a free community newspaper originating in the heart of the Labour movement and bedrock socialism yet open to all, and distributed these days to 10,000 homes in West Cumbria. Egremont Today in its turn owes its existence to one man, Peter Watson (with Connie his wife never far away), and if anything this collection is a tribute to him, to his compassionate heart, his faith as a Quaker, and simply what I would call his obsessional genius (he acknowledges the obsessional bit!).

Peter, as editor, constantly requires us to reach out into and beyond our local communities to any who have been sidelined, sidetracked and are likely to go unnoticed and unsupported. He is unflagging in his affirmation of all sorts and conditions of humankind: he seeks the potential for creative goodness in every human being, knowing how far we all fall short. In this enterprise he has encouraged me to keep putting my bit in, believing that community life needs to focus on the spiritual life (in all its aspects) as on the needs and hopes contained in the mind/imagination and the body. So be it.

My aim in writing Godspot has been quite simply to say on the one hand to church people and other regular worshippers of all faiths that the God we seek to believe in is almost certainly different from the God we think we believe in; and to say on the other hand to those who see themselves as unsure, put-off, agnostic, atheistic, Christian but don't like organised religion, and spiritual seekers out there, that there may be more to this God business (and to the Christian idea of God in particular) than you may think.

I am deeply grateful for the opportunity over the years to explore spiritual horizons hopefully in words and stories that people may see through more readily and may lead, for some, nearer to the Truth of our being alive at all in our amazing world. Remembering that each person's journey, arising out of our common humanity and the shared circumstances of our lives, is nevertheless unique.

Acknowledgements

Technically I am a latter-day dinosaur. I live in my cave and have emerged from time to time with my inkpen in my hand to write another Godspot.

My thanks go out to many people. First and ever foremost to my wife Sheila without whose patience in putting everything I have ever written and crossed out and rewritten onto computer, Godspot would never have seen the light of day.

Also now to Jane Holmes who with boundless enthusiasm and immense computer savvy has shaped this into bookform – and enjoyed the work!

To family member Emma Soulsby who arrived with the many faces of Man and Woman for the cover.

To Edna Branthwaite and David Scott for permission to use their poems.

And to encouragers who have said "Godspot is the first thing I turn to". "I'm relieved you wrote what you wrote"; especially to Allan Holmes and Bob Brydon who with Peter Watson have persistently urged me to select some to make a book.

To the 'hidden ones', all the volunteers who cluster round Egremont Today month by month to make it happen at all – reporters, sub-editors, photographers, other contributors and those who go out and about in all weathers to get it delivered.

Inevitably to Peter Watson who has constantly felt Godspot to be 'the fire in the belly' of Egremont Today and has urged me on month by month when I was hesitant about putting more words into print. He has also facilitated all the printing of the book via Egremont Today.

Many quotations are difficult to trace. If I have inadvertently breached any copyright in the publication of this book I apologise and will set this right in any future edition.

(I am a retired Anglican priest who spent his last years in full-time ministry in Egremont, West Cumbria).

David Wood. – Autumn 2009

Introduction

God's Hotel

A flourishing hotel is full of comings and goings, people usually with a clear sense of purpose, people on their way, experiencing life in the making or unmaking as they move from one place to another. So there are arrangements, expectations, consequences - there are business agendas, holidays to take hold of, meetings happy and sad, celebrations, reconciliations, humiliations, final farewells. Dreams are on the way, betrayals are exposed, promises made and broken. There's a lot of baggage around, of every kind. It's a constant collision of small and individual worlds where people are blind to anything really apart from their own bit of life - get me into here, get me out of here.

There are smart staff too, keeping their eye on you. Certainly there are standards to keep up, so you can't let everyone in for there are those around who undoubtedly will lower the tone of the place: it's a wide definition of course but 'guests' need to be acceptably smart. Money anyway is the international language and a good looking credit card works wonders. The patient staff will not allow you to loiter without intent for too long.

God's Hotel is rather different. The commissionaires are all girls and boys about ten years old, beggar-orphans who come up to you, take you eagerly by the hand and come in with you, whilst a legless beggar scoots past on his wheely-trolley up a gentle ramp which stretches right out into the world: the presidential suite is a fun palace for the disabled.

All are welcome. There are no foreigners. Nothing has a price-tag. Here you are allowed to be whoever you are, wherever you are in your life. Anxiety, fear, drops away as you enter - so hoodies arrive in their gangs and quite soon their heads come out and they smile around finding their weapons meaningless.

Here are the overlooked, the politically incorrect, the dazed, the amazed, the doped, the deranged, no one is short of attention. Boozers, pickpockets, yes smokers, cheats and frauds, muggers and buggers all there if they want to be; the bad and the ugly alongside the truly good, whoever they are. It's a potent mix.

Prostitutes find that inside they can rest as equals, unharassed they don't have to stay on the game anymore. There are the stonking rich all around laughing like drains because they have learnt to give it all away. Here the blind teach the sighted to see and the deaf help those who hear to listen. The only people who can't get in exclude themselves because they can't face leaving all their baggage about other people behind. This may be heaven but it's not a kingdom, rather a place where the power and violence of prestige and good standing have no meaning, influence no reach. Welcome to Godspotting.

May my heart lend its ear to every cry of pain
like as the lotus bares its heart
to drink the morning sun.
Let not the fierce sun dry one tear of pain
before I have wiped it from the sufferer's eye.
But let each burning human tear
drop on my heart and there remain
nor ever be brushed off
until the pain that caused it is removed.

(Gautama, the Buddha, 4th Century B.C.)

OUR HISTORY, OUR STORY

Valentine – February time, anytime

It's playtime. It's gushing, full flowing Valentine time. It's torrents of love time pouring out and over (it's highly expensive roses time!), it's the impossible quart into a piddling pint pot time. Yelling out, yippeedeedoo time! It's deep calling to deep beneath the noise of the waters. Ecstasies, extravagances, everyone's a poet time. Remember Julie Andrews – 'The fells (well hills! I suppose) are alive with the sound of music'.

It's suddenly innocent time again. Silly? Pull yourself together, trim down? Rubbish! We are forever pulling everything in tight. It's as if every time we have something beautiful and romantic and flourishingly abundant to shout about, to blurt out or send across the wires in flowery or naughty code, instead we grit our teeth, clamp our lips firmly shut and sink back into our thermals.

No! Valentine is the ancient statement from the dawn to the end of time. It's at the heart of us all, longing for release. Someone to say I love you to or to hear the words back 'I love you'. It's our destiny. It's the ache of reaching out, it's the gladness of being held, whether you're friends, or lovers, or just holding hands.

So reader, you think I've turned into a March Hare - well, a February Hare. Gone mad with nonsensical passion eh? So what's the matter, are you in the middle of a great freeze or something? Come on, unhook your hat. Has your loving become like an old woolly, have you got to be careful all the time? Gone into my second childhood have I? No, recovering my childhood.

That's the wound of the world, that we think this sparkle, this marvellous clarity of innocence has gone for ever. Our first innocence is dulled over perhaps, winded. Hurt certainly, but not gone. It is playtime, however screwed up or old you feel - whether you're 15, 25, mid-life critical or 150. We were made to play, we were made to be love makers, to live in the oooooooos and aaahs and the wriggles of delight.

The World Community for Christian Meditation International Centre

"The important aim in Christian meditation is to allow God's mysterious and silent presence within us to become more and more not only a reality but the reality which gives meaning, shape and purpose to everything we do, everything we are"

-John Main-

**INTERNATIONAL CENTRE
CHRISTIAN MEDITATION RESOURCES
ST MARK'S, MYDDELTON SQUARE,
LONDON, EC1R 1XX, UK**

www.wccm.org

mail@wccm.org
Tel: +44 (0) 20 7278 2070
Fax: +44 (0) 20 7713 6346

Opening Prayer

Heavenly Father, open our hearts to the silent presence of the spirit of your Son. Lead us into that mysterious silence where your love is revealed to all who call. Maranatha...Come, Lord Jesus.

How to Meditate

Sit down. Sit still and upright. Close your eyes lightly. Sit relaxed but alert. Silently, interiorly begin to say a single word. We recommend the prayer-phrase, 'Maranatha'. Recite it as four syllables of equal length. Listen to it as you say it, gently but continuously. Do not think or imagine anything-spiritual or otherwise. If thoughts and images come, these are distractions at the time of meditation, so keep returning to simply saying the word. Meditate each morning and evening for between twenty and thirty minutes.

Closing Prayer

May this group be a true spiritual home for the seeker, a friend for the lonely, a guide for the confused.

May those who pray here be strengthened by the Holy Spirit to serve all who come and to receive them as Christ himself. In the silence of this room may all the suffering, violence and confusion of the world encounter the power that will console, renew and uplift the human spirit.

May this silence be a power to open the hearts of men and women to the vision of God, and so to each other, in love and peace, justice and human dignity. May the beauty of the Divine Life fill this group and the hearts of all who pray here with joyful hope.

May all who come here weighed down by the problems of humanity, leave, giving thanks for the wonder of human life. We make this prayer through Christ our Lord.

We are meant to be as little children inside, laughing and leaping within whatever the weather outside. We are meant to be trailing clouds of glory. Unless we become as little children we cannot enter the kingdom of heaven. To refuse to play is to refuse our manhood and womanhood. It is to stand joyless outside the gates of life, always. Go on, ruffle one another's hair. Be lavish.

I once went to a family where there had been yet another row. There they were, he was sitting gloomily staring into the fire and she was back on the settee, looking like a whipped dog. After a bit I asked him "Do you love her?" "Course I love her". "Do you ever tell her?" I said. He said "Oh she knars yer knar". It was the one thing she didn't know anymore and longed to hear.

Yes! we were all innocent once, remember that. Not born sinners as some tub thumpers say, just born into a devious and disordered world. Look at the old photos. The laugh in a baby's eyes when love is true. There were days, many days that were carefree, when the skies were open and the clocks stopped. We trusted so much, oh! how we trusted. Easily happy, easily hurt, big forgivenesses came readily like water from a tap.

The innocence is still there, lying perhaps forgotten like buried treasure. We can heave off the burden of experience and return to it. This does not mean to be infantile or childish but to be childlike. To allow warmth to flow in deed and word, love. To unsour our bitter eyes. To trust our feelings of goodness again. To dare. Even in our small circle, there is need for constant reassurance, for delightful surprises, for fun. For playtime. Creation is meant as a playground, not all grit and graft.

If, after all, you're saying, "I'm too old for all this sort of thing", I'm sorry. And if you're saying, "What's all this got to do with God?" I'm even more sorry.

Even so, I love you, Peekaboo - yours leaping greenly, Brer Rabbit.

P.S. Centuries ago there were two nuns in a convent. They really disliked one another intensely. They never spoke. Even so, every evening when one sister returned from chapel the candle in her cell was always lit.

Omagh-August 1998

It is a glorious Saturday afternoon. And here I am, aged 68, marvellously high in the sky, high on High Spy, over Borrowdale, looking away down over Derwentwater to Keswick, with the great wind and the cloud and the sun all chasing one another on this splendid summer afternoon. With me my so-precious wife and greatly loved step-daughter and her magnificent husband. What a time, what a day to be alive! We, the golden oldies, have huffed and puffed our way up from Newlands Valley. The wind is mighty, huge. Hang on! we are being blown to bits. And because I am not following Wainwright's golden rule which is, don't walk and look at the same time, - (stop, then look) - I tread awkwardly on a slate which bounces up and gashes my leg. Blood all over the place. And some panic, too, because it is my 'not-quite-right' leg. A moment of high drama. Will it stop bleeding? Can I walk the X miles to the car? Not a stretcher, surely! A swift handkerchief, tightly bound, and we continue. Soon the laughing again, some skipping of the downhills and when we get happily home the cut is the size of a thumbnail paring - a joke really.

At just that time on that high and happy hill, in Omagh, Northern Ireland, 28 people were blown to bits. Blood all over the place.

(About the same time a year earlier give or take a few days Diana, the Princess was killed. And each of these twenty eight was equally a prince or princess in their own right, in the heart of their lovely lives and in the eyes of their beloved families),

I hope it is not too hard for me, for you, to go back to that time, and place. To August 15th, 1998 at 3.10p.m. For us to go back there together, where the wounds will never heal and the blood of so many lifetimes will pour out without staunching through the lives of those who remain living.

So many human beings continue to murder one another. This harvest of evil. How far back are we prepared to travel inside ourselves to see that this begins in our own hearts; that it is not first and foremost a hatred of others that has done this, but a hatred of ourselves? We hate others because we hate ourselves more than any other living creature. So many of us carry within a cancer of self-loathing. If you doubt this, ask any of our teachers about the children who come in through the school doors. We learn that the only way to survive, the only way we can live with ourselves, face ourselves, is by taking it out on others. Pretending it is 'them' not us. We declare war on peace. 'I have', someone wrote, 'the germ of all possible crimes, or nearly all, within me'. As we look inside we see only a barren land, a tale of poverty and starvation. An interior wilderness of cries that were never heard. The wells that should be filled with ever fresh springs of love and compassion, are cracked cisterns, empty, dry. So 28 people die. And just over the world, in Kenya and Tanzania a few days earlier, at the American Embassies, nearly 10 times as many die in another grisly, desperate nightmare.

The evil in the world must be uncovered in our own hearts. It is there, it has to be recognised and evaporated so that the superior essence which dwells in each one may rise to the surface and slake the ugly thirsts of our lives. There is perpetual sunrise to be found in every human heart, always there ready to dispel the darkness of our self-loathing.

So it becomes a time of remembering, deep within, the prayer of someone who loved life so much, and for whom any life was so precious, that he, or was it she, could hate no-one to death:- "Peace to all men of evil will. Let there be an end to all vengeance, to all demands for punishment and retribution. Crimes have surpassed all measure. They can no longer be grasped by human understanding. There are too many martyrs. And lay not their sufferings on the scales of justice, Lord, and lay not these sufferings to the torturer's charge, to exact a terrible reckoning from them. Pay them back in a different way.

Put down in favour of the executioners, the informers, the traitors and all men of evil will, the courage, the spiritual strength of the others, their humility, their lofty dignity, their constant inner striving and invincible hope, the smile that staunched the tears, their love, their ravaged broken hearts that remained steadfast and confident in the face of death itself.

Let all this, O Lord, be laid before Thee for the forgiveness of sins, as a ransom for the triumph of righteousness. Let the good and not the evil be taken into account.

And may we remain in our enemies' memories not as their victims, not as a nightmare, not as haunting spectres, but as helpers in their striving to destroy the fury of their criminal passions."

(A Jewish prisoner in a concentration camp).

So 'Egremont Today' is 100 months old and getting younger all the time. Congratulations to all who week by week, month by month, carry out the huge routine chores and do the footslogging to get it out onto the streets and in through the door. All dreams need such dedication to make them real. Come true.

For 'Egremont Today' is born of a dream, a vision - of making community. It's about helping people to see one another, to hear one another, to share what they have, their gifts, and belong together. Like it? hate it? change it? shape it?-join! Interdependence. It's only by learning to reach out to others that we grow straight and tall, become independent ourselves and fully human. It's only by being together that we set each other free; you cannot be fully human without other human beings.

All a far cry from those harsh voices who have told the nation 'there is no such thing as society'. No such thing as the common good? That is blasphemy against the human spirit because the human spirit is a sacred, holy place where by belonging together we learn what it is to be godlike and discover the divine inside every human being.

So all are included - not just the healthy and strong, the creative and obviously talented (and thank God for them) but those around the corner from us for whom life has become a prison, a drab sham. People shut away in a corner. The dream includes those who are pushed down, trampled under, who live crushed lives under a great weight of oppression. Those whose voice has become so enfeebled that it cannot be heard. May not have been heard for generations. The dream is about lifting all people. Up into laughter and shouts of joy. 'I belong'. 'I have a place'. 'Somebody cares'. 'I am welcome and needed'. 'I can do things, I have gifts'.

And the dream reaches out across Copeland in West Cumbria to all the world. Yes, charity begins at home, but home is as much a place we are going to as a place we have come from. Home is a dream you have to travel to and build.

All this in these few monthly pages? Yes. Precisely. From seeds in the garden, mushroom lasagna, to transcontinental roadways and beyond. From burnt African places to the drenching of a Lakeland summer. From natural 'gurners', through the happiness of children, the enquiry and adventures of the young, the poems of the sad to the bleak refugees of the world's orphans. From our street to your street, from here to there, from there to everywhere.

So here's a story, one that Jesus told, to celebrate this good event. You might not like it, but it is the world community as it's supposed to be. It is The Dream.

A farmer wanted workers to help him get in the summer harvest. At the beginning of the day he went out to labourers who were standing there, agreed a wage for the day and sent them off into the fields (that's how it used to be in Cumbria. Farm workers would gather at harvest time in the village square and wait to be hired by the farmers, a day at a time).

Going out some time later the farmer saw others standing there, waiting, so he said to them "Go and work in my fields and I will give you a fair wage". Off they went. He did the same at regular intervals during the day. As evening started to come in and there was just an hour or so left before the light would fade and the work would finish he went out once more and still there was a further group standing round. "Why have you been hanging around idle all day?" he asked. "Because no one would hire us" they said. So he said, "Off you go into my fields".

When they all came to be paid after work was over, the farmer paid everybody the same wage, the last as well as the first. There was an uproar. He said to those who had worked all day "Take your wages and go. I have given you what we agreed. I choose to pay the latecomers as much as I pay you".

Those who had been left hanging around all day were those nobody wanted - the sickly, the disabled, the weaklings, those with learning difficulties - the 'poor specimens'. Always the strong, the vigorous, the well-favoured, would get chosen first. Real community is a bit of heaven, where no one is excluded, where all are equally favoured and a place is found for them with all the others. Their place. Their unique and equal place.

Here's to a double century - at least - for 'Egremont Today'.

<u>Remembrance 2000, two Minutes silence for…..?</u>

Stand straight. And still. Bare and bow the head. Lay your wreaths. Salute if you are military or feel that you must. Sound the Last Post. Let the notes silver and keen their way through the thin November air. Lower the flags. Keep the silence lest we forget. We will remember them. We will remember them. But remember who, going through our daily lifetimes which we can only live once?

I remember Jake and Rachel, my grandchildren, starting full-time school one September time along with countless others. There had been so much anticipation by their parents and the little ones. Imagine across the country all those homes buzzing with excitement and a little fear as the first day draws near. All the preparations to start doing something which it is their right to do. Which school even or where? My daughter and husband living in Dubai, had to replan the whole thing, and re-jig some complicated holiday arrangements in order to be back for the first day at school, discovering at the last minute that in this Muslim State, schools start on a Sunday not a Monday,

Jake in his first-day school uniform, mischievous and proud. That first day, a big threshold to step across into a brave new world of high professional integrity and the deepest child care. Jake, after a few months only, already transformed, quite as bright-eyed, doubly bushy tailed, alert to living, and ready to learn all that there is to learn in this world.

How many died in the two World Wars of the last century? between say 50 and 70 million? Yet this year across the world, 125 million children will not even start primary education. 'Universal primary education could cost £5 billion a year, roughly what is spent on armaments every four days, or rather less than the USA's annual spending on cosmetics or Europe's on ice cream'. 125 million is equivalent to all 6-14 year olds in Europe and North America. (Encounter, July 2000).

Child abuse? This is universal child abuse of epidemic proportions which we all condone because we grow fat as a people and nation on the armaments trade and ice cream. We grow fat off the death of children, (another 1p on income tax for 'this sort of thing'? Not on your life, not on their lives).

Stand straight. And still. Bow the head. Lay your wreaths. Sound the Last Post. Lower the flags. Here indeed is a war for modern times, here indeed is two minutes of deep silence to grieve over. Lest we forget. Lest we forget. Here is a war we don't even know how to, don't even bother to remember.

Here also then let the anger rise, feel the passion in the gut. Here also let the marching on the streets begin. For life without primary education is as good as dead, and the fall out from such a lack is appalling. Two-thirds of young children not in schooling are girls, and one in four girls who start primary education drop out within four years. More than half of the women of sub-Saharan Africa are illiterate, yet basic education substantially improves lives. The child of a Zambian mother with primary education has a 25 per cent higher chance of survival than the child of an uneducated mother. In the Philippines, a mother's primary education reduces child mortality by a full 50 per cent. (Encounter July 2000). In Uganda 4 years of primary education will raise a farmer's income by something like 7%. And for a poor farmer that can mean the difference between hope and despair.

International debt remains a major obstacle. In 1997/98 Tanzania paid 4 times as much in debt repayments as it spent on primary education. Teachers cannot be paid. Schools close.

In 1990 The World Conference on Education for All pledged primary education for every child by the year 2000. By 1995 that target had become 2015. And where is it now? Betrayal is one of the things that happens in war. 'And we have been betrayed. After all the fine words and good intentions, the G8 leaders who met in Okinawa, Japan in July 2000 (costing £500 million, the richest summit ever) have gone back on their promise that the year 2000 would give a new start to the world's poor.' (Cafod/Christian Aid).

Think of your children and your children's children and keep, I pray you, two minutes' silence before you move on.

<u>Foot and Mouth</u>   —   May 2001

So......after the banner headlines, after the holocaust of foot and mouth in Cumbria and the mass graves, after the procession of broken faces and families day by day before us, now the empty pastures and the silence of the land. These terrible things. Who can imagine what it was like for the farmer who spoke quietly and sadly that his livestock would have to be slaughtered - "In two days time I shall wake up, go out into the farm and there won't be a sound". And all the lovely people who make their living from visitors and were looking forward to preparing their welcomes.............

"I feel there is a curse on us" one good church-woman said. Another - "Perhaps this is a punishment from God". Curse it may be, punishment it may be, but one thing is certain, it is not from God.

We have brought it upon ourselves and the innocent and others are all involved. Indeed the riddle is that we are all to blame and no one is to blame. We must however all accept responsibility. It is our land, our buying and selling, our farming industry, our tourist trade, our economy. If other people are our brothers and sisters, never was it more so than now. One world, one family, one acceptance of common fault: the now famous exchange between a farmer who confronted two people crossing his land who said to him, "This outbreak is nothing to do with us, we're vegetarian" is pitiful.

We find ourselves caught in a trap we ourselves have made, unwittingly, partly through greed, partly through ignorance and illusion about what we thought we could do that we could not in fact do.

If you want to describe 'sin' this is it. Sin is a consequence of thoughtlessness, unmindfulness, of not knowing what we are doing, what we are getting into. And often we get caught up in current trends, which exploit others, to do the best we can for ourselves and our families. We catch each other out. Exploitation is always evil. It is difficult for the individual to be farsighted and strong enough to be different, or even to recognise what exploitation is.

Of course most farmers cherish their livestock, have feelings towards things that breathe and eat. But we are all driven - farmers sometimes against their will - to buy quality more cheaply. We all want to get more for our money and sometimes cut corners or cheat quietly 'as long' we say 'as it doesn't harm anyone'.

It always harms someone though it may go unrecognised.

The supermarkets have a huge responsibility and we love them - a bargain is a bargain, an eye for an eye. Successive governments bear a huge responsibility and that means us, the people. In the end the government is the people. We elect them (or neglect to vote, it's the same thing). We have turned the blind eye, fudged the issue.

What has happened is that we have lost the plot. All life is sacred, the Earth and all that is in it. That's the plot we have become ignorant of. This is the terrible price. All animal life is sacred, it is against this we have to see the holocaust of the animals, a desecration of life, that we have participated in these last weeks, perhaps our worst times of national history since the end of World War Two in 1945: this is not to be sentimental, stroke Dolly the sheep, cuddle the cow or melt inside at the sight of a lamb; no, we grow them for food, for profit, to sustain our family lives.

But their lives are sacred and when the time comes for them to fulfil their present destiny (which is to make food for us) they need to be treated with dignity and due reverence. That is why the RSPCA prosecute farmers who neglect their livestock. And instead we have seen such things, thousands of animals tossed frantically into scrapheaps of fire. And yes, I have to say I love chicken and accept without much thought the appalling battery conditions in which they are reared and slaughtered and prepared for my table.

We love to worship a Consumer God and indeed we are now being consumed. We are being eaten by our own greed and thoughtless desires; our live now, pay later culture. If we had looked far enough ahead of course we would have tried to learn and prevent what has happened.

19

What about the 'real' God people pray to? One thing we must grasp, God never punishes. God never curses. That God is out of the window, was never there except in people's imaginations. It is we who have made such a God, blaming God for the consequences of our own unmindfulness. God can only forgive. God cannot punish. This is love's true nature. This is how God intervenes, with forgiveness, always, God is only ever compassion.

Our grief is the grief of a God who suffers with us. Our despair rests in the heart of God. What God loves is for us to perceive our errors and mend our ways. People behave badly and have to live with the consequences because we have forgotten that we are good. That is our true nature. Not bad, good. And God - closer to us than we are to ourselves - is there to remind us to lift our heads, leave guilt behind and try again to move on as best we can, with a sense of the sacredness of all life always in our hearts and minds, always before our eyes.

INTERLUDE
Flanking Sheep in Mosedale

All summer the sheep were strewn like crumbs
across the fell, until the bracken turned brittle
and it was time they were gathered
into the green patchwork of closer fields.
Dogs and men sweep a whole hillside in minutes
save for the stray, scared into a scramble
up a gully. A dog is detached; whistled off
by the shepherd who in one hand
holds a pup straining at the baling twine
and in the other, a crook light as a baton.
His call cuts the wind across the tarn;
it is the voice of the first man, who
booted it across this patch to bring
strays to the place where he would have them.
You can tell that here is neither love nor money
but the old game fathers have taught sons to win.
It is done well, when the dogs lie panting,
and the sheep encircled dare not move.

(David Scott - a national poet and one time vicar of Torpenhow,
Cumbria)

<u>Honouring Cumbrian Farmers -</u> July 2001

Soon, if not already, Cumbria will be backwater news lost in the dust of a general election. Just like so many other times and places of disaster around the world. Not an earthquake perhaps or a typhoon but they are our sufferings here, which will drag along in heavy days long after the headlines have gone.

Little things and big things. The eggs that cannot be sold because no one has come to eat them. The silent streets and lanes. Bed and Breakfast hanging its empty sign out onto the equally empty road. Pump sales are well down. And the ice cream makers, and hirers of boats and bicycles. Closed shops. Hotels with one eye shut. Jobs down the tube and businesses to the wall, homes and livelihoods shaking in their foundations. Tourism bleeding in a hundred places: some communities taut as fencing wire with conflicting interests and so many lost and cancelled opportunities.

And the front line - for that's what it was - the huddled hedgerows of dead beasts. The day the MAFF came with their Dalek commands just 24 hours before they stopped slaughtering healthy cattle on adjoining farms. You saw him perhaps, our representative good husbandman farmer, standing there, grieving at a whole memory of years obliterated in a moment, 'beautiful Belgian blue heifers all ready to calve' (if only it had been 24 hours later). The craft and graft, the sheer satisfying ordinary glory of hard work, year on, year on to get things robust and healthy and good. It's like coming home and finding the house burgled; the place desecrated, violated, cheapened, raw. Your farm, your homeplace, your good fettling-place, despoiled.

The stories will go on and on, reverberating across the fells, down the sheep meadow, through the village landscapes and pleasant towns of this good land. This good land. It is right that they should. Tell and tell again. These generations will not forget. The imagination of farm children and their families will live in flashback never quite forgetting, never quite resting easy; certain things they will never avoid seeing, certain places that will always breed an inner sickness. The jolly chattery passerby visitor of years to come will know nothing.

It has been just like a war, a plague that blitzed family and community life. The confusion of a nation unprepared. It's always the same with war, we ought to have seen it coming and we didn't and there out of the blue, is the killer, at your back gate, over the wall. A virus of snipers, taking you out when you were not looking or despite every vigilance. Where will the enemy strike next? Casualties. Some panic. Getting overwhelmed by the odds. Hasty, messy planning, especially in the early days. Some stupidity. Always the same in war, wrong decisions, tragic mistakes and miscalculations which only aggravate anger and the uselessness of it all. The waste, always the waste and looking for someone to blame. Choices all the time between evils; nothing perfect and clean. Everyone gets hurt. And the black smoke and the smell of rottenness and decay. Just like war.

Yes, and in the middle of it all always the opportunist on the make, some cheating, lying, turning a blind eye and doing quite well, thank you, out of the suffering and carnage. The rest of the nation has no idea.

So, in honour. In just one small corner, two West Cumbrian farmers I knew, working a family farm a hundred years old. Gentle giants. Massive hands. They'd been all day up the fields lambing and it was almost dark. That early dark of late winter. And now lumbering down the fell they were knackered, when out of the corner of the eye they spotted what looked like 'just like a snowflake' on the bare cold ground. They went over and gathered up the little white scrap, 'she fitted into my hand'. They took her into the house, kept her in a cardboard box with an electric light bulb to keep her warm. (A story repeated again and again across our fells). Day and night, early and late, day after day, they fed and nursed as she gathered strength and bleated and wobbled into some sort of life. Always on the watch, always guarding; such respect for life. Until the day she could get up and out with the rest. They were so quietly proud to tell the tale, and how she became a sturdy breeder over many seasons. Part of the family and such a landmark in their farming life that there on the kitchen wall up against the fireplace was a panel picture embroidered by their sister, the sturdy full-grown 'yow' in good colour and underneath, 'Snowflake'.

And when one of the brothers died suddenly, sadly, the graveyard was black with some hundreds of standing-around farming men in mourning who had come from all over, as they do, and couldn't get into the little country church.

The story goes on. Here I have to be more personal but the Reverend Joe Johnson of Calder won't mind because he told the story about himself so often, and to those who knew this ancient man, once shepherd, then priest, he was a local saintly hero anyway.

It was at this same funeral and Joe was to speak because he knew the family well. A difficult occasion. The church was stuffed with those broad-beamed men and women, into narrow pews. As they sat hot and tense, not quite knowing how to be at such a sad time, Joe began:- "I've always got on well with farmers, except one who wouldn't give me the time of day. He was in hospital so I went to visit him and I couldn't think of anything to say. So I said brightly trying to make conversation – "I was a shepherd once" - and the farmer replied, "What was the matter lad, couldn't yer mek it pay?""

The human heart is resilient, and the determination is that through all the suffering better things will grow - though we cannot yet see them - for the land, for the animal world, for the people.

Meanwhile, it has to be said, at the villages of Beit Jala and Beit Sahour, known as the Shepherds Fields, just a few kilometres from Bethlehem, the gunfire and the killing continue.

9/11

11th September 2001. We will remember those images of death exploding into our watching eye until our dying day.

I have to say that this collection is not meant to be read as a novel. Sip rather than gulp. It's not meant to slake your thirst but stimulate your appetite. The original pieces were not written like that, they just came month by month offering some comment on our times. So dip in, switch about, read one or two and put down. Go back again later. Then the godspotting will be a nudge here, a wink there, to keep the reader in touch with a bit of reality.

There is a story in the bible which somehow seems very relevant. It is about the building of the Tower of Babel (Book of Genesis Chapter 11 vv.1-9). From a sermon by **Rev. Dr. David Edwards** at St.John's, Keswick - 16th September 2001:-"Why have men throughout history delighted in erecting tall and solid buildings? Here - 5,000 years ago - this tower ironically was in Mesopotamia, modern Iraq (the tallest tower in the world today is in Malaysia, another Muslim country). A ziggurat. It is a symbol of human pride and power, of men aspiring to be God (v.4 'a tower with its top in the heavens'.) It is a symbol of the desire for fame ('let us make a name for ourselves'). It is a symbol of the illusion of security ('lest we be scattered abroad upon the face of the earth')". Footnote 2009 – the tallest tower in the world is now in Dubai.

Then **the Dalai Lama:-**
"This is the moment of your ministry. This is the time of teaching. What you teach at this time, through your every word and action right now, will remain as indelible lessons in the hearts and minds of those whose lives you touch, both now, and for the years to come. We will set the course for tomorrow, today. At this hour. In this moment. Let us seek not to pinpoint blame, but to pinpoint cause. The message, we hear from all sources of truth is clear. We are all one. That is the message the human race has largely ignored. Forgetting this truth is the only cause of hatred and war, and the way to remember is simple - Love, this and every moment.

So, talk with God today. Ask God for help, for counsel and advice, for insight and for strength and for inner peace and for deep wisdom"..........................."That is the challenge that is placed before every thinking person today. Today the human soul asks the question: 'What can I do to preserve the beauty and the wonder of our world and to eliminate the anger and hatred - and the disparity that inevitably causes it - in that part of the world which I touch?'"

Dr. Jonathan Sacks, Chief Rabbi:-
"Optimism is the belief that things are going to get better, hope is the belief that together we can make them better. So I believe that hope is precisely what we, as religious leaders, have to offer the world by joining together to make things better".

Kanan Makiya, an Iraqi dissident now teaching in the U.S:-
"The problem is deeper than bin Laden. The disease that is in us, is from us and within us. Against this kind of enemy the West can do nothing. We have to do it ourselves. Muslim and Arab have to be on the front lines of a new kind of war, one that is worth waging for their own salvation and in their own souls. And that, as good out-of-fashion Muslim scholars will tell you, is the true meaning of Jihad; a meaning that has been hijacked by terrorists and suicide bombers".

A Muslim student at The London Business School:-
"Don't *fear* us. Don't patronise us". A mild grin. "And don't call us towel heads".

Messages from America
Samara Joldersma:-
"I think we often in this country have somehow felt like God's special little sunbeams - exempt much of the sorrow in the world and we have often gone merrily and unconsciously on our way with little regard for the rest of our planet. I have sometimes felt we really seem to think we are the main occupants on this planet and what is left over is OK for whoever else may be out there".

Cheryl Sawyer:-
"We became one colour.
As we carried each other down the stairs of the burning building
We became one class.
As we lit candles of waiting and hope
We became one generation.
As the fire-fighters and police officers fought their way into the inferno
We became one gender.
As we fell to our knees in prayer for strength
We became one faith.
As we whispered or shouted words of encouragement
We spoke one language.
As we gave our blood in lines a mile long
We became one body.
As we mourned together the great loss
We became one family.
As we cried tears of grief and loss
We became one soul.
As we retell with pride of the sacrifices of heroes
We become one people".

Deepak Chopra:-
"And I ask myself, why didn't I feel this way last week? Why didn't my body go stiff during the bombing of Iraq or Bosnia? Around the world my horror and worry are experienced every day. Mothers weep over horrendous loss, civilians are bombed mercilessly, refugees are ripped from any sense of home or homeland. Why did I not feel their anguish enough to call a halt to it?"

And some lines from 'America the Beautiful' by **Katharine Lee Bates** - 1913:- (sent by **Samara Joldersma**)
'O beautiful for glory-tale
Of liberating strife,
When once and twice for man's avail
Man lavished precious life!
America, America
God shed his grace on thee,
Till selfish gain no longer stain
The banner of the free!'

Yet another war looms. By the time you read this it may well have struck like a viper's tongue. As a world we continue to lurch from one holocaust of suffering to another, a ceremonial burning at the stake of another largely innocent and powerless nation of victim people; at the stake of human greed and lust wielded by the powerful few and often wrapped up in a cloak of moral righteousness or even worse religious justification. No one is clean.

One of the gravest perils of fuelling the dragons of war is that at base level, at ground zero level, behind the political front doors, there are innumerable and influential hangers-on who bring with them the basest of human motives - to be top dog, to rule the world, and to glean the richest pickings.

Faced with the proven evil of Saddam Hussein something has to be done . The sad reality is that this time round we may yet again have to resort to violent means. This is where we are stuck in the history of the world but we have to grow away from Violence. We have to grow up from Violence. We have become besieged by Violence. The violence of wars and counter-wars, of worldwide terrorism, violence on our streets. No one feels quite so safe anymore and fear is rising.

The media can never leave Violence alone, day by day they assault our sensibilities, picture after picture, item after item, usually, but by no means always, just doing their duty. From A to Z, all the way from Afghanistan to Zimbabwe, calling in where the murdered young are desperately discovered, at D for Milly Dowler and S for Soham on the way. Every letter of the alphabet will tell a violent tale.

So what do we do? Well, we can take to the streets in our thousands with high and handsome placards for Peace not War. We can have peace vigils, go to church to pray for peace and come out feeling better as if we have done our bit. But as ever it starts in our own backyard. All the protests and prayers are in vain unless, at the same time, we face the violence that each of us carries in ourselves. There is no other way to world peace, and this is usually where we stop, we are all such cowards.

For we all have huge reservoirs of anger, impatience, hatred, dislike which eke out in mean judgements and petty bitterness everyday of our lives if in no stronger hands-on way. We constantly practice unforgivenness, unrelenting miserable condemnations. So often we give no quarter and are bilious towards so many different sorts of people. Think only of the people you 'cut dead' (aye, there's a phrase). We already have our lynch-mobs (Soham again, Bradford, Oldham race-riots, homosexuals, and (suspected only) paedophiles). If we step back and say this is not me, dress it up in more congenial words, then we are fooling ourselves. We buy violent toys. We condone violent video-games. We hate when our team gets beat.

The Church of all places should make a difference. By the Church I mean the people who want to be known as Christians, not the institution. The People can make a difference but Christians have to realise that the gospel we are supposed to live is a non-violent gospel. Yet 'Christians have often not made a difference and at times the difference they have made has not been Christian'. (Joseph Komonchak). The blessing of nuclear submarines and other engines of war has nothing to do with that gospel.

If we want to be upfront about being Christian then we have to be prepared to do 'the work' in our own lives, painstakingly facing each local, tiny personal situation from family values to supermarket checkouts and traffic delays - and deal with the violence we find erupting within. That's where the world of peace starts. Think of the twentieth century and the trillions of peace prayers that were offered on the one hand and the mounting escalation of violence and wars on the other. We never start small or local enough. With ourselves.

A man on a cross is a signpost for everyone. Crucifixion is a horrific death by violence. The Jesus-symbol is that you, me, each one of us absorbs violence by embracing it with love. Love inevitably means some suffering. Sometimes a lot. It usually means dealing with our own selfishness. That is 'the work'. Not idealistic, simply the truth that everyone knows in their heart of hearts. It begins with me. On my street. With my neighbour. That's the way world peace will grow and the fangs of violence be drawn.

Iraq and praying – June 2003

There's a lot of it about. 'Oh my God! praying people'. There's No. 17 dancing around on the touchline as if he wants to go for a pee, crossing himself and muttering something to go with it (watch my lips) desperate to get on the park. Massed marines all looking at their boots as some chaplain prepares them for battle. The solitary haunted rookie waiting to go into the next Iraqi town, to say nothing of the families and congregations back home.

Churches in recent weeks have been loading up with vigils, special acts of prayer, and in city churches and cathedrals which are open all day, rather more people than usual popping in for a few quiet minutes. Even Jeremy Paxman at one time dared to pop the question about prayer to none other than Mr. Shining Light Blair (a world leader who actually goes to church and reads the bible, but don't tell anybody because it might embarrass the Labour party or put the voters off, which is why I'm putting it in brackets so that you won't really notice). And as for Mr. President and those White House mornings which begin each day with prayer, well - yes indeedy, there's a lot of it about, even though there are those who can't resist sometimes saying, 'it's an emotional crutch, superstition, people who pray haven't grown up, etc. etc.'.

The fact is that most people (60%+)in these sceptred isles pray at least in private though they may be embarrassed to admit it; and in times of great peril feel the need to turn inward or look outward in the hard faith that there is a power around bigger than us which is there to help. When the pressure is on, people want to feel that they don't have to face the anxieties and uncertainties alone.

So what actually is prayer? It can be anything - a shout for joy, a whoopee to the world, a cry of distress, a call to be more alert and come safely through danger. It can be an explosion of anger at the unfairness of it all (Frank, full of health and wealth celebrating his ruby wedding and impending retirement on Saturday, dead by Tuesday), a looking for a way through, a plea to be sustained through situations of unimaginable horror, a resting, a silent listening. Prayer is the desire to believe that through it all somehow 'all shall be well and all shall be well and all manner of things shall be well' (Julian of Norwich, our earliest English woman saint). Prayer however does not bring us any closer to God. It's not whistling God up - 'hey you there Lord of Lords,

30

have you a moment? Over here'! Prayer is a reminder that God, Universal Love, is closer to us than we are ourselves. It is a desire to open ourselves up to this continuity, this Beyond that runs through the whole history of humankind and through the centre of all of us. The River of Life. The Golden Thread. The Indwelling Spirit. It is there, Presence, always. It is Being, the vast universal engine of Life.

'To be or not to be?' How 'to be' in this situation or that is the recurring question, the recurring prayer, all down the ages. True prayer is not just out of the mouth......'Ourfatherwhoartinheavengabblegabblegabble'. It comes out of the depths, out of our gut, our heart. And it need only be short-'Help'. 'Thank you'. 'Oh my god'. 'Jesus' 'Allah be merciful'. The Spirit is so close, it knows our needs before we ask. True prayer often comes with terrible sighs or bursts of delight too deep for words. It is a need for silence, for rest, for reassurance.

Prayer can so often feel to be very private, individual, isolated. In fact we never pray on our own. The same prayer gathered together by the power of Being (God) is being expressed by thousands of human hearts across the world that same instant in a maze of different circumstances. The words don't matter. The language doesn't matter. What matters is bending to the power of Being coursing through every single body. In worldwide -web language - this site has just had over a million hits! Our solitary prayer is gathered up and expanded into an immense solidarity, yet my prayer remains unique because it is growing out of my own life and experience.

It's like driving down a narrow country lane and you are the only car for miles, then suddenly coming into the dense volume of traffic as you descend onto the motorway, all piling along in the same direction. You seem to be very small in your own metal compartment but your place in it with all the others requires your unswerving alertness and best attention. Yet you are part of a flow. The wise ones say - 'If you want to pray, God will give prayer to the one who prays'. The way to learn what prayer is, is not to read about it but do it. There's a lot of it about. There could be much more. God (the secret of Being) is hidden and has to be discovered by each one. That is prayer. If God were to show overwhelming proof of Presence, that would take away our freedom.

Tsunami, Desperate Times - February 2005

Tsunami. Some ask - why did God not intervene to prevent such appalling human misery? Because there is no such God. Some say - it is God's Will. With every respect to the many millions of religious people around the world who believe this I have to say rubbish, there is no such God. People who profess any belief in 'God' or a 'divine principle' at the heart of all things have to face up to these brute facts, sooner or later.

Listen to the language we still use in worship - 'Hear us merciful Father, we humbly pray....' 'Look with favour on your people', 'Remember Lord your Church in every land..' This absentminded God who has to be pleaded with, implored, constantly tapped on the divine shoulder to remind 'him' about us all, does not exist. We persist in making 'God' in human image only, a dressed-up superhuman, an occasionally benevolent eye in the sky, and this is woefully inadequate. Our God is pathetically small. We have to take the words of Rowan Williams, Archbishop of Canterbury, and breathe them into our souls – "God is different from any kind of difference we can think of or imagine as different".

People of faith have to learn to survive in the pounding, chaotic seas of doubt and contradiction. We have to leave behind such images of God. We have to wake up and grow up. Tsunami, amongst all the other things it is and is not, is a wake-up call to 'believers'. We have to live at a much deeper level in the black-dark mystery of faith. Nature is beautiful, it is paradise islands, it is fertile, abundant, bursting with life and colour. It is also red in tooth and claw.

The astro-physics of the universe now tell us that we are living on a knife-edge all the time, that the chance of life at all on planet earth is so finely calibrated that it is like passing through the eye of a needle in all the permutations that could have happened in the evolution of our world. That is the miracle if you want it, that there is life at all. If you want to talk about 'God', some physicists say that 'the divine principle' is evolving in us, in human beings, all the time (it is 'love' that makes the world go round, love in us and through us) that sheer goodness is at the heart of all things and has to be uncovered; that this is the human quest, the ultimate purpose in life. And as many have said in these last days, if you want to discover 'the divine principle', 'God', in what is happening, look at the response of the peoples of the world. Unprecedented. Amazing. Almost beyond belief that we should care so much, reach out so far.

Be certain therefore amongst all the dark mysteries of the universe which we have not yet comprehended and seem to defeat us, that the volume of goodness, of sheer unconditional, unrelenting love is expanding all the time; the divine principle is emerging gradually in hearts and minds. There will always be large corruptions, exploitations, perversions, evils to spiral us downwards towards despair, but look at the proliferation of people caring for people in recent generations - not only globally, Oxfam, War on Want, Christian Aid, Cafod, Water Aid, Unicef, Amnesty International, but in our own backyard - Mind, Shelter, Help the Aged, Alzheimers Society, Alcoholics Anonymous, Samaritans, Stroke, Scope, RNLI, Hospice at Home. And then there is Rape Counselling, Debt Counselling, Bereavement, HIV/Aids Counselling. Drug Rehab, on and on the brilliant list goes.

At heart, people are magnificent. We are magnificent. All the time we are coming further out of our shells; climbing out of survival ourselves, we look to help others survive. This is where we have to put our faith in these desperate times when faith is sorely tested. In the great religions of the world, unperverted and undogmatic, there are central teachers, who, in the way they have been amongst us, show us the way to balance the human and the divine in our living. Suffering is part of our quality of life, it happens. If we run away from it when it hit's the fan, we destroy ourselves and others. Through the suffering which comes to us we can be moved into a larger and larger space which embraces more and more people. It is very hard. It is also the truth. Pray? Why of course because prayer is an intensifying of light into dark places, a focusing of our collected goodnesses which nothing can blot out except our own blindness: let us not be afraid of the power of our compassion.

Tsunami is a large moment in human history, we have in a few days enlarged our human horizon. We stop eating, we look, we stare, we weep, our hearts break, we reach out, human barriers dissolve. It is a new world alright if we want to make it so. Hold onto this large moment, lest we forget, in the months ahead when the horrors recede and we are sucked back into some of the greeds and meannesses of daily life, and when we go into the snarling infighting (we need to grow up here too) of the next election which will sicken us. Lest we forget. We are in our heart of hearts, magnificent, so much larger than we dare believe, and this in the end is the only thing that matters.

"............You've just got to get on"

I have lived amongst old dying industrial communities all my working and retired life. And mining families have coloured me through. The first was a Welsh miner who had walked 5 miles to work to start a 12 hour shift at 6.00a.m., and then at 6 in the evening walked the same 5 miles home, day after day. There he is lying a-bed, this great Hewi of a man, sick with a breathing that will not last much longer. His tiny wife, white hair all a-frizz, is wearing one of his old double-breasted jackets - the points trail the ground. I am there as a priest because they want communion. Sprightly as a new day, she whips the clothes back, plumps in alongside her man, saying "will you have me luv?!" Which was the more sacred moment, what I had brought or what I had witnessed?

Six dead pits on which a new town is being built in the 1970s! A woman remembers how as a child with 5 siblings, she walked home one and a half miles from school for her midday butty. The dolly tub was ready for her and she possed away until it was time for school again. So small, she had to stand on the stairs to use the dolly at all.

A woman twice married and after 7 years both men dead. After that married life - no children -was over. (I have lived 14 married years in retirement in addition to all that went before).   She heard about the first death from the woman selling oranges from the cart in the street. Then, there was Granny Hart and the four children, and the day he never came back................... "you've just got to get on".

So many mining families crowd my memory. They have given me so much with their solid courage and deep, deep humility. Just to be with them. Always ready to share what little they had left ("can you lend a cup of sugar pet?") and be there for others in their turn. Mercifully and unwittingly, time and again, they cut me down to size.

Here are a few words from life in West Cumbria amongst these amazing, ordinary people.

Miners' Song

Songs from the shows now,
anything goes now
to make a solemn music
in this land of granite worship.
Momentary spasms of joy perhaps
from straining alleluias
brief as a winter sun;
a hurdy-gurdy of holy songs
leading - then - the choiceless generations
out of the church
back to their pit-black homes
and the flickering alleyways of their stunted lives,
all prepared for an early dying;
as meat for the Christmas oven,
the Christmas moment of the manger words,
"Save us, born to die".

All journeys led below the ground.
"Give us this day our tunnelled bread",
black bread, bread of life bread,
little bread at that
and not many circuses.
The early falling eventide
masks and abides a diminishment of lungs
heaving their way out of another
night-filled day.
This was the miners' fare,
blasting the rock of countless ages
in the hope it would 'cleft for me'.
Small wonder hymns are slow and sad
with their weight of empty memory,
so many fortunes lost and lost
and lost again.

Only the names remain
of bright philanthropists
plaqued on the chancel wall
and above each street,
propped up as they were
on their pit-prop wealth
while the earth trembled.
Above ground names.

INTERLUDE

Inheritance

They lived just off the poverty line,
Yet left me riches to last a lifetime,
I cannot thank them now for gifts they gave,
The treasures they bestowed were not
Paper and pennies to be counted and hoarded
But the simple commerce of the countryside.
He taught me where to look and find
The primrose's hoard of tumbled gold
Lying hidden in banks of green.
He gave me old hedgerow names
Like Mother of Thyme, Thrift,
Bleaberries and soldier's buttons.
She gave me a wealth of words
That came easy to her mind and lips
Despite her basic schooling.
I struggle to make beginnings and ends meet,
To fill the breach with words
That can only be reached in the mind.
They left me history and lineage,
A bounty of deep and binding roots
That hefted me to Cumberland.   ©Edna Branthwaite

'Hefted' sheep are flocks who down the generations have been bred to
wander and survive far and wide on the Cumbrian fells.

Edna responded with this poem. Her father was a miner and she grew
up in a mining family. There was so much simple beauty in the heart of
the mining community.

TIMELESS – THE LABYRINTH

Timeless – The Labyrinth

This is a Labyrinth, a very ancient symbol. All cultures and religions throughout the ages have produced them, ranging from simple spirals to complex twists and turns. They are not mazes designed to trick or fool you with walls and dead ends. They have no barriers and only one way to the centre and the same way out. Some are small, no more than a few yards across; others cover many acres. But why on earth? What's the purpose? From the 13th century pilgrimages were hugely popular and the labyrinth was a sort of 'virtual reality' pilgrimage site for people to come and use who were not able to go on the real thing. Christians used them to help them deepen their sense of prayer and meditation on the divine: this labyrinth is a copy of the one found on the floor of Chartres Cathedral in France and is regarded as the finest in the Christian world. And just as today such pilgrimages are increasingly undertaken (Lourdes, Mecca, the Holy Land, Compostella, Iona, etc.) so there is a revival in labyrinth making and walking. And in case you think this is all very honky-tonk American and 'new-age' there are several labyrinths in West Cumbria. Why not follow the path with your finger or a pointer, take a bit of time and pause here and there to reflect on your life and think about things.

Silence and Stillness - Slow time

Is God Here? That is not the first and most important question for someone struggling to believe. The first question is - Am I here? For our ancient forebears, the Celts, God was immediate, here, around, everywhere, in and through everything, now. The mystery of God's presence was on the doorstep, nearer than that. If you read Celtic prayers they have a prayer for everything:- opening your eyes, putting on your clothes, 'smooring' the fire, cutting the peat, scattering the seed, drawing the water, walking through the mist, milking, shearing, sailing.........................

All our religions have this sense of the nearness of God in them but in our times we have dressed up our religion too much in words, we have talked God out of court, made God a book of rules, pushed God into the mind, shoved God at arm's length: like births, marriages and deaths, Sundays and sickness, like you would call in a solicitor or doctor or garage mechanic if the car broke down.

Not a God who is always around and alongside like a good friend. Not a God who breathes in us, not a God you can praise if you go to the toilet well (like St.Julian of Norwich, the most beautiful of English Saints) - oh no my dear, nothing like that!

Perhaps experience of God - for those who are looking for it - is hard to find because we are looking in the wrong place. So much of the time we are not in the here and now ourselves. Many of us spend so much time either in the past or in the future. We are either going over what happened, wishing for the good old days, regretting what we have done, reliving old successes, trying to cover up our mistakes; or planning ahead, deciding what to do next, wondering how we shall fit it all in, wishing it was time off, or shall we be able to afford it? We are constantly distracted from the here and now, rushing through today from yesterday on the way to tomorrow. We are frequently moving so fast doing things now, in order to get onto the next thing. We gulp food down in order to............It's a gallon into a pint pot, let alone a quart. We want to be doing everything because we think that is 'really living'.

But God is not in the past, nor in the future. Here and now is all there is (ask anyone who is recovering from a severe illness or accident). Eternity, actually, begins here and now, it's the only place you'll find it, not in a golden spot beyond the horizon. But we think we have to wait for it because we are not living in the here and now. More than this, we have become conditioned to being distracted (to rush from one thing to the next) so that if we are not distracted by the next thing or interminable action replays we don't know what to do.

Suggest to people that they sit, just sit, for five, ten minutes, a quarter of an hour, even, I dare you, half-an-hour sometimes, and do nothing - just Be Here - no planning, no calculations, no viewing, no I'm-doing-this-because-it's-good-for-me - and hear the screams – YOU MUST BE JOKING!

There is a verse in one of the ancient poems in the bible - 'Be still and know that I am God'. It can be calming and strengthening to find a five minutes to be still for awhile and say that over to ourselves - quietly, over and over.

Try to find such a space from day to day as you can. You might have some surprises as bit by bit you have that special slow time and centre in on yourself. Others have. All through history.

UP CLOSE AND PERSONAL

<u>Silence and Stillness - Rhubarb</u>

'Rhubarb, rhubarb, rhubarb'. There's just not enough sitting under The Rhubarb Tree. That's a big part of our troubles.

When I was in a drama group and learning about acting there were sometimes scenes where the principal characters were front of stage doing their stuff and some of us were in the background having to talk or comment amongst ourselves, words the audience never hears. I was taught not to have a proper conversation, but just say 'rhubarb'. It is important that you are there rhubarbing away (meaningless though it may seem) for you are part of the story, but you are just to be still, waiting, not in the limelight, not drawing attention to yourself. Doing nothing, yet alert and aware of the main action.

Rhubarbness is learning to do nothing well. It's a discipline about stopping.

Here's a Rhubarb story, true I'm told. There was an exceedingly busy Catholic church in London. Lots of people all the time. 400-500 at certain midweek services. Three priests stretched to the limit. Comes the time when one is to be moved and cannot be replaced. How will the two left cope? Their cardinal asks to see them – "There's only one solution" he says, "you will now have to take two days a week off instead of one".

Do, do, do. Busy, busy, busy. Useful, useful, useful. The hundred and one activities, some of which are necessary, many of which we have chosen, swirl in and around us. We blow our cheeks out, we complain of the pressure - there are just not enough hours in the day. It's almost as if unless we can complain of not having enough time for ourselves, we feel as if we are not alive. 'I must be doing something', so often the cry.

We also need to do nothing. Not just grow the flowers, but smell them. Not doing is as important as doing. Part of our troubles is that we have lost the art of loitering without intent. We need a discipline of stopping - we need to learn again to be still. Babies, young children have it marvellously. They are playing full tilt and then suddenly switch off, stop. "Where's she gone to then?" you ask. She's gone to a real place.

She is being still in the heart of herself. Not centre stage but backstage - rhubarb time. Meaningless time in so far as you cannot measure it with activity or usefulness. It doesn't seem to move things on and yet................

We need Rhubarb time. We need time that cannot be measured by output. We need still time. A discipline of stopping. Why? Because otherwise we lose the perspective of who we are. We need to keep rediscovering within ourselves our own horizon. Each of us has a different horizon and it changes as we move through life. It is sub-human to allow ourselves to be totally driven by activity from day to day. It's as if we have become afraid of stopping, of being still.

People are like pools of water. Splashing in the pool may be fun a lot of the time but it muddies it up. When we are still the pool settles, becomes clear and we can see into its depths. Often there is such beauty there. Things never noticed before appear. Nothing to be afraid of. They are there all the time, part of us.

Sometimes I walk forest paths. We chatter as we go, breathing noisily, then someone will say 'just a minute'. We become still. And in a little we become aware of sounds and movements and colours and smells that our noise had obliterated. They were there all the time, a huge world, part of us and our walk.

We need time to be still. No clear picture comes out of a shaky camera. Rhubarb time helps to give us all the time we need to come into balance between doing and not doing. It is also being gentle with ourselves and that's important too. Rhubarb time helps us to see how small we are.

Small does not mean unimportant. Small is good. Too bigness, ego, is a killer - that terrible death-rattle in the throat of one who at the end of their life says -' if only I'd had more time'.

<u>She loves you, yeah, yeah, yeah...!</u>

In Charles Dickens' story 'Nicholas Nickleby' Smike is a crippled, utterly wretched scrap of humanity. Abused, despised, orphan-abandoned, he is treated with contemptuous cruelty by those to whom he was entrusted to look after him. They will use him as a slave until he drops and then they'll discard him. That most terrible phrase - 'they couldn't care less'.

Until Nicholas arrives, who puts his arm round his abject misery, shields him, becomes his champion. Calls him 'friend'. "Nothing", Nicholas says, "nothing will ever separate me from you". Smike doesn't have to do anything except be Smike. And from feeling utterly unwanted, an outcast, you watch Smike, start to smile and hope, surprised by joy.

Surprised by joy. The same happens when you are truly in love (remember? all you golden luvvies). To be truly in love is to be surprised by joy. She wants me, he wants me-of-all-people. It's not just that she's got the hots for me ('I lerv your body!'); she/he wants all of me, every fibre of my being, inside and out. And it sounds like she wants me .... forever!? Well then, I say to myself, but it won't last, as soon as she finds out what I'm really like, that'll be it. But no! she wants me, all of me, just as I am. She wants to be with me all my life to come, every living moment, for better for worse. She/he seeks me out, texts me, phones me, will wait for ever till I come round. ME? Funny old screwed up me with all my cliff edges for her to fall over - if only she knew.

Yet somehow she does know and it doesn't matter. I'm wanted after all and I don't have to do anything to prove it, to show I'm any good. She believes in me. No wonder I'm wild with joy.

People feel the same when God is somehow revealed to them. God they discover is personal, is a Who who has been waiting for them for ever and will wait for ever, until they turn and see. What they discover is that God delights in them even more than parents delight in their new born child. It's personal. ME? I am wanted by God? Little me, in this vast universe? Indeed, that is how it is and any other pictures we have of God are less than God. God's wanting us is absolute. God's delight in us is unconditional. It's not like Kitchener's Call to Countrymen in the 1914-1918 war with a ferocious face and a heavy pointing finger at you to which millions gladly , yes, gladly, responded and went on and out to untold suffering. One of the singers of songs in the bible says speaking for God, 'Even if the unthinkable happened and a mother forgot her children yet I will not forget you; your name is engraved on the palm of my hand'.

God's wanting is outpouring every nano-second of time. God's delight is within time, sustaining all of it, all of us. It is we who mess it all up and still God's delight is undimmed. Nor will it ever be dimmed, through all the sadness and griefs with which we respond. The energy of love at the heart of it all is too massive, so far beyond what we can understand; yet it touches us, is personal.

Archbishop Rowan Williams :- "God thought 'Let's have a Milky Way!' Then he thought 'We can do better than that; we can have intelligent life, and failing that we can have human beings!' And God thought it would be interesting if human beings were diverse. 'What I would really like is a Rowan, a Sarah, a Daniel, an Amal, a Youssef, a Selina, a Mohamed, a Ngawang and so on and so on. I long for there to be someone to receive my joy in a way that no other person can'".

The whole of Creation is wanted and delighted in by God. It is easy to get stuck in the cynical and distrustful cycles of our present world, and in a Church which has also very often become jaded and weary, and to forget the original joy and wonder which is forever waiting just at hand to be recovered. Life is amazing. It is all too easy to forget that every moment thousands upon thousands in every corner of the world, of every faith and language, are being shocked to the core of their lives by the revealing of a presence we call God who wants them as indispensable and unique, as a vital part of creation. A God who delights in declaring in their inmost spirit, 'I am your friend for ever'.

Mindfulness or Who do you think you are?

Mindfulness. 'Give us this day our daily mindfulness'. I went to a teaching day once with the splendid title 'Meditation - a Way of Unity for all peoples on earth'. We thought the day was going to be about grand universal themes like world peace, the fellowship of humankind, the harmony of the universe, etc. But the leader would not let us get past 'me', 'you', 'I'. She said quite simply that there is no point in moving onto the larger stage unless at the same time we are constantly seeking to be at unity with ourselves; unity within is where it all starts. To come to peace in our hearts with who we are and what we are.

Eleanor Roosevelt, one of the authors of the Universal Declaration of Human Rights, made the same point. Working for human rights does not begin out there in Zimbabwe or China or North Korea but it begins she said in 'small places, close to home'. I guess close to home can feel too close for comfort. What's going to happen if we keep examining ourselves? Is all we are going to find a can of worms, Pandora's Box, the uglies? Well, there is that, we have to face up to it, but it goes with the territory of being a human being. Come on, we all have some uglies, some of us very uglies, yet if you want a decent meal there comes a times when you just have to face the pile of dirty pots in the sink. And as you tackle them, behold they become clean (the fairy stuff doesn't do it all on its own, you have to become hands on - even with a dishwasher.)

There is much more to all of us. Unless however we become reconciled with our bad bits, we shall never release the far greater goodness that each possesses; we shall be forever limping instead of walking tall. We have to learn wholeness, practise it. 'Mindfulness' is a Buddhist practice (no! the word 'Buddhist' does not mean 'real Christians look away now'). Rowan Williams, the Archbishop of Canterbury says that when the day of judgement comes, the crucial question we will be asked is not why were you not Nelson Mandela or Mother Teresa but why were you not Rowan Williams, David Wood?

There was a bishop in ancient times who rose to great eminence in the world. He became known as Arethusa the Wise. He quite liked that. His counsels were widely sought, he was honoured everywhere and his life became full of pomp and circumstance. He came to die and was somewhat disconcerted to find himself standing shoulder to shoulder in a vast crowd of people before the gates of heaven. An archangel came out and announced "This is a roll-call. When you hear your own true name called step forward and enter". And so it began. As name after name was called, person after person stepped forward through the gates. Arethusa the Wise expected that he would be amongst the first but this was not so. The crowd grew smaller and smaller until eventually he alone was left standing there. He advanced on the archangel and demanded "Why has my name not been called?" "Oh", was the reply, "your own true name was called a long time ago but you did not recognise it when the moment came".

'To thine own self be true'. This is why daily mindfulness, a daily examination of who we are and what we are is so important. A Quaker, Pierre Lacout, wrote, "Give us each day our daily silence". It's the same thing. To make a space - it need not be all that long - for personal reflection, looking at our motives, our good loving, our failures. Otherwise we are forever running away from the first great central task of living which is to come to unity in our hearts.

We owe it to ourselves, we owe it to everybody else.

Oh yes, I've said this before but then we are so forgetful, we so easily lose track and direction, we are so easily distracted. We need constant re-minding. Such reflection, also, is prayer. It is, in old fashioned but necessary language, calling our sins to mind, what we have done that we ought not to have done; what we have not done that we ought to have done. Perhaps our daily forgetfulness, our lack of mindfulness, is our only real sin.

Native Indian, Cherokee wisdom:-

"Worthy performances do not make us who we are, but little things and what we tell ourselves in the privacy of our own minds. We are what we are and what we believe is important. We are children to the end - innocent in ways we do not understand, aware of our spiritual connections and afraid to develop them. What would people think? How will I explain that I no longer enter into those activities that are thought so clever? There's a world of things we do not have to explain. As much as we want others to understand and like us, if it takes us off the place where we need to stand in a world of unlikely places, then we flirt with disaster. No one can dictate to us if we are not listening. We will not lose our footing if we are not teetering. We are who we are by what we choose to cultivate, and all worthy performances are made up of very little parts".

Wounded Healers

We are all wounded people. In some way. Griefs, sadnesses, slights, betrayals, lies, missed meetings, love not recognised, indifference, blindness, accident, cheating. Part of life is always sorrow.

Quite often we wound or are wounded, not deliberately but with the best intentions. I am one of a whole generation whose parents were taught that it was best for babies to feed them regularly and systematically just once every four hours, no matter how much they cried in-between. Apart from anything else it was supposed to teach discipline and obedience at an early age. My parents did their best for me and to hear me crying on my own in my cot would hurt them dreadfully. I think I was just a very hungry baby. My son needed feeding every two and a bit hours. Innocent wounds. And in those days children were taught to be seen and not heard. No wonder I became a clergyman - getting up in the pulpit and getting my own back.

Our whole culture is a negative put down culture which says never give praise because you only make others bigheaded. What nonsense! We need reassurance always and our gifts need honouring. This bestows self-respect. The mind games of conceit, arrogance are only putting yourself on a pedestal and boosting your ego to avoid being seen by others as you see yourself. Weak point, shout loud. Bully, bluster, your way through.

The echo-voices of the world are legion - you're ugly, worthless, nobody - NOBODY - unless you can prove yourself somebody. In many ways we seek to hide our wounds to avoid rejecting ourselves totally. Even if we are a 'success' it is surprising how, when things go a bit wrong, we are soon tempted to give way to the lurking monster within - I'm no good, unlovable. Isn't it true that certain hurts come back to haunt us time after time after time?

We are wounded people. We all have many failures, as a normal part of life, but how were we treated when we failed? With courtesy, encouragement, forgiveness or with cold mockery and a turning away of faces? Who first made you feel small? Things happen that seem very big to us, yet to others they seem quite slight. Who first gave you the pull-yourself-together-routine?

One lad comes running into his mum with a bloody knee. Oh my goodness! High drama. To the rescue. Warmth and cuddles. He tumbled on the path and grazed his knee. Another lad in another place in another town also comes running home, crying hard and holding his knee which he says hurts. But there's not a mark and he can't get the real words out, that he slipped in the road and the car stopped just in time. Mother rubs the knee and offers words of comfort. "There, there, it's not so bad. Look, nothing really. Come on, cheer up. Nothing to worry about. You're fine".

We are all wounded people. But go gently because our wounds can become our gifts. Who do you think answers the telephone at Samaritans? People who know how other people hurt because they have been hurt themselves and have not turned away from their wounds. Who runs refuges for battered wives? Battered wives, turning mindless brutality into the dignity of caring for others and nursing them back to life. Bereavement counsellors are usually those who have been bereaved. All these know the territory. They wear their wounds with honour, get to know them and discover they are gold. These strange contradictions bring forth so much beauty at the heart of life that an experience which seemed like an enemy can turn into a friend.

Love your wounds. Love yourself. Get help if you need it - there are many good and patient wounded healers around.

There was once a King who had a wondrous, magnificent ruby. It was a joy, the source of all his wealth and power. Every day he would gaze on its lustre. Then one day he noticed to his horror that it had become scarred by a scratch. All the palace jewellers were summoned but their judgement was that nothing could be done without causing further damage. The King was devastated. He offered a great reward and jewellers came from far and wide, but all woefully said the same thing. Nothing could be done.

Then a servant came forward in fear and trembling and said he had heard of an old retired expert in jewels far away in the hills who was supposed to be gifted at working with damaged gems. He was sent for and in due course a shabby old man shambled into the palace. The whole court glared with scorn at this nondescript – "You're wasting your time, majesty".

Even so the King showed him the great ruby and the old jeweller said "I cannot repair it. But if you wish I can make it more beautiful." More contempt, more laughter. The King though, was desperate so the old jeweller took the ruby away. A few days later he returned and placed the precious jewel gently into the King's hands. Carved upon it was the most delicate rose, the scratch transformed into the stem.

Calling people names

Labels. Labelling people. You might almost say libelling people. They are this sort of person, those sort of people. You look across the restaurant at the much older man and the much younger woman snuggling into food in one corner, and you spin your fantasy story. Or, on the beach, you hear someone being very big and bossy in a foreign language, and you say "Hmm - an X . Typical, they're all like that".

I had this conversation recently in one of the local shops. I go in and the shopkeeper asks "Been away?" "Yes" I say "to France". A customer [C] chips in "Would never trust a Frenchman. Stab you in the back as soon as look at you". Me: "Met any?" C: "Ooo lots". Me: "Where?" C: "Oh everywhere". Pause then C: "They're just like the Welsh".

When we meet people we don't know, one of the first things we often do is ask the question. "So what do you do?" And when you get the feedback – 'I work in a bank', 'I teach', 'I'm a tinker, tailor, candlestick-maker', you slot them into your frame of reference by labelling them. You put them in your place - for them........ 'I might get off with her' or 'No way'. 'Labour? Tory? Lib.Dem? Greens? - politicians! Oh my God! And as for BNP, well!' When people discover I'm a clergyman I watch their expressions change.

A look appears on their faces like 'Is there a bad smell around here?' (did I say something I shouldn't have?)

Labels. A sad bit of labelling I hear is the one some women put on themselves – "I'm only a housewife!" I once had to ask a woman her occupation for the baptism register and she replied, "I'm a domestic engineer". Brilliant!

Labels. It's a sinister practice. A visitor to Ireland turned a corner and suddenly found a gun in the back of his head and a voice saying, "Protestant or Catholic?" Quick as a flash and all of a sweat he said, "I'm a Jew". And the voice drawled, "Well, aren't I the luckiest Arab in all Ireland"!

Labels, lumping people together and refusing to wait and discover them as precious and different individuals, breed war, pestilence, famine and sudden death. Labels conceal fear and hate. Nigger! Jew!

During preparations for D.Day in the 1939-45 war, an English woman wanted to be hospitable to American troops She wrote inviting six of them to tea, and demurely said – "But please, no Jews". At the appointed time there was a knock on her door and she opened it to find six black soldiers – "There must be some mistake" she spluttered. "No maam," said one of them "Colonel Cohen never makes mistakes".

Labelling begins with you and me in our own backyard as we trundle to and fro on our daily doings. It is one of the most evil things we ever do. When we do it, we practise evil. You may not want to hear that. It may make life easier to put up the barricades between ourselves and other people in this way, to practise this shorthand, but it is the high road to misery. We are continually selling ourselves and others down the river with this perpetual self-deception. The fact that like attracts like is no excuse. 'It doesn't do any harm' - I hear the limp lettuce reply.

Wrong! It creates havoc, it is our evil. It's like spraying an aerosol slogan over 'those people'. Like on a Maryport wall – 'All coppers are dickheads'.

Religious people are no better at it than anybody else, which is why so many people are put off religion and God. Yet all religions say that the only way to bring peace and harmony and justice into our lives and so into the world is to practise walking in the other's shoes. God is already there.

There is only one cause of evil in the whole earth – "Mine is the only view that matters".

The Good Book (Bible) says 'Anyone who says, I love God and hates (labels) his brother is a liar. Since a man who labels the brother, that he can see, cannot love God, whom he has never seen'.

One of the Buddhist teachings says – 'By oneself alone is evil done: by oneself is one defiled. By oneself alone is evil avoided: by oneself is one purified. Purity and impurity depend on oneself. No one can purify another'.

INTERLUDE

Jesus went to a football match between Catholics and Protestants. The Catholics scored first. Jesus went wild with excitement, cheered, threw his hat in the air. Then the Protestants scored. Jesus again cheered madly, threw his hat in the air, laughed with delight. "Hey, you", said someone next to him, "whose side are you on?". "Oh, I'm not on anyone's side" said Jesus, "I'm here to enjoy the game". "Huh!" muttered the other one to his neighbour, "an atheist".

Bodies

A word about bodies. The August holidays are a time when there is a lot of exposure of bodies wherever we look - travelling, queuing, sprawling on beaches, splashing, dashing bodies; bodies cycling here there and everywhere; bodies upfell downfell, canoeing, feeding, yahooing, (tired children - and adults), setting your stall out for a catch...... It all goes on. Bodies. Your body. My body. Magnificent, not so magnificent. Able, not so able. We are what we do with our bodies. They are the most sacred possession we have.

And as bodies Brits are amongst the elite of the world. Most of us can choose what we do with our bodies, and for those who can't there is increasing support to help us make the most of our limitations. In many parts of the world though, from sheer perpetual endless hours of grinding labour to the desperation of sex-workers, children and adults have no choice but to have their bodies exploited (as once it was here).

So where are we? "The body tells us the truth as nothing else can. It expresses our way of being in the world and our attitude to others. It can be no more than an object we sell or exploit, a sign of desperation. Or it can be a possession whose appearance and well-being we become obsessed with, a reason for living rather than a means of living. It can be a bridge, a means of mingling our identity with that of others. Or it can be a castle where we raise the drawbridge and keep the enemy at bay. A sacred thing or fetish". (Laurence Freeman).

The universal wisdom of all spiritual traditions is that the body is the Temple of the Spirit. The whole world we have made has emerged from the heart of that temple. The future of the world stands or falls by our use or abuse of our bodies. Our learning how to live in balance, in moderation, is for the cure and healing of all peoples. On holiday many will visit churches/temples/sacred places (especially when it rains). They may visit a beautiful building and find it lifeless within - 'it left me cold' (exactly) - or inside they may discover something very alive, a warmth, a vitality, a beauty and a wonder, much more than they bargained for - 'I'm just gobsmacked'. Though the architecture may be worn and crumbly.

And that's how people see us clothed in our bodies. The body may be made up, patched up to be beautiful, plasticated, nipped and tucked, yet the eyes are dead: or a body may look and sound worn out, nothing to do with age or illness, but rather like a car that has been run right into the ground without ever being cleaned or serviced. But I have a picture on my wall of an Indian woman who is beautiful. She is quite aged with a face all rough and dirty, full of the hard work of life. Yet a smile, a wisdom crinkles out, and she has long been a guide and mentor to me. She is like many faces I have seen knocking about in the ex-mining and heavy industrial communities where I have lived. 'Soul' that's what it is. Due attention has been paid to the sheer beauty within, our own sacredness. Don't be afraid of your soul, no matter what other people say or do.

Warts n' all

One day as I came from what I can only describe as a long bout of praying in church one of my children said to me "Tell me Dad, why is it that all that time you spend praying doesn't make any difference to the way you are at home?" It was a show stopper! Our children can be our most penetrating critics. And family rows have been punctuated down the years by the comment 'why don't you practice what you preach?' How many of us have heard that one?!

I also remember when I was once having a particularly hard struggle with myself and trying to talk it through with a bishop. I said, "I feel as if I'm two people in one body sometimes, a real Jekyll and Hyde". There was a long pause followed by a sigh from the bishop who then said, "Join the club". Then he went on to remind me that some of my gifts which he also saw, arise out of the parts of me that are not right, damaged if you like. My gifts which are just as real are the flip side of the coin called 'me'. I am quite certain that I am not as God intended me to be, but it's not either/or. I'm not either horrid or holy, it's both/and. I am both a Horrid Henry and a Holy Harry.

Yet I flourish and am allowed to flourish. The contradiction at the heart of any life is that, if we are aware of them, are open to them, our flaws can be turned into gifts, our weaknesses into joys, indeed into strengths, happinesses.

And that's how it is. I am a flawed being. We all are. Not as God intended, not as real Love means us to be. Part of me will never be right, my flaws, such as I know them, are my perpetual companions. Yet they can be changed into glory and that is also my experience of myself and others. Fancy a person like me feeling called to be a minister of the Church. What a nerve! Yet I know my weaknesses have been part of the reason why the Church has continued to accept me.

DNA, genes, are parts of me that cannot be changed, much as I might wish it. I am as I am. It's part of the mystery of me. Indeed they are not there to be changed but, if I am aware of them and honour them , are there to reveal to me truth and beauty and goodness. Perhaps also to some others.

The whole of creation is damaged. One way or another. What is amazing is what people make out of their limitations. Deformities beget great kindness and great heroism. Blind people do indeed see. The deaf do hear, the dumb do speak; and the lame do leap for joy. Not as I leap, but they leap. How they leap! It is so. It happens. Beautiful music comes out of the most unlikely people.

So, homosexual relationships. Many gay men and women are homosexual, not because they choose to be but because that is how they are and they cannot change as they please. They are not perfect, they are damaged just as I am and you are, only in a different way. That becomes the frame for their happiness and fulfilment.

And the whole Church is in a real mess about this. For centuries, out of ignorance and prejudice, the Church condoned slavery. For centuries the Church condemned Jews until growing human experience interpenetrated the Church's teaching (based on the scriptures) and honesty had to prevail.

Bishop Spong a retired Anglican bishop has campaigned all his lifetime for honesty in Church affairs and teaching what we actually believe; indeed to bring into closer focus what the Church preaches and what it practices. "We have had hundreds even thousands of gay bishops in Christian history. We have also had homosexual popes and homosexual archbishops of Canterbury. Do church leaders really believe that closeted living covered over by lies is a virtue?" He points out, "Cultural differences between the first and third worlds are enormous. There is no western nation that would allow women to be treated as they are in many parts of the world. In Africa the spread of AIDS is rampant because the culture of many parts of that continent proclaims the right of males to have multiple sexual partners".

Finally, he pleads, unity based on The Bible "is not about God reconciling different points of view among church members, it is about God in Christ reconciling the world to God. If that is the task of the Church, then the Christians of the world and their leaders must face both their ignorance and their prejudices in the light of truth and reality".

The Dark Night

'It was a dark and stormy night and the rain came down in torrents'.
And it actually was, one February up on the Northumbrian coast.
An evening service with a bit sing, a bit talk and a bit pray.
Afterwards this woman came up and said "Thank you, I've been
waiting 15 years to hear that" 15 YEARS! to hear what? What I had
talked about was 'The Dark Night of the Soul', a place so deep
inside where every person who wants to take the Christian life
seriously must be prepared to arrive at. It's when pretty well
everything you thought you believed about God and Jesus doesn't
mean the same any more and starts to disappear. Religious
structures in your life disintegrate little by little. Words which
before meant so much become empty and tasteless. A whole swarm
of questions we had never asked before emerge. As a Cumbrian
clergyman I know said a year or two ago in computer language "It's
as if the screen has gone blank and nothing, nothing I can do will
bring back to life the words and pictures". That is the Dark Night
when all that is left is sheer faith, sheer holding on.

What that woman did not know was that it's par for the course, part
of the journey. She thought it was all her fault; she was doing
something wrong, had lost it. That's terrible. She did not know that
to grow into the Christian God the images of God out there will
become blurred and start to vanish, to be replaced it seems by all
the hobgoblins and foul fiends of our doubts, mistakes and failures.
They rise up to rage us, faced as we are by our self-righteousness
and lack of mercy. She thought God had gone off and left her to her
own devices (15 YEARS!) She did not know that she was
becoming more her true self, more Godlike; that the sense of
divinity, instead of being out there at arm's length, was growing in
deep intimacy within. She was living an increasingly
compassionate and caring life but did not see it as God's presence
growing in her. 'I have no hands but yours, no feet but yours'. She
may have said the prayer but did not believe it.

Alone and fearful in the heart of a dark night when you feel utterly lost is a terrible place. All the lights have gone out. She was so relieved to learn that bewildered and directionless, she was yet on the right track. Her faith was immense - 15 years! Relieved to know that she was not alone and that it could just be that God was nearer to her than when she first believed.

This is the individual story for so many, part of the personal journey through life. It is, simply and completely, about taking risks with love. What we have to grow up and recognise is that where we are now, as a world-people in these dark, dark times when violence and abuse are increasingly exposed, is that we are all together in a Dark Night of the Soul of the World. There is an increasing agony and compassion in many, many hearts. That compassion and agony is Presence. We have to hang on: to hold onto the beautiful and good, to hold onto the heart of our dreams come what may. It is each individual's responsibility (this has happened before through human history and it can happen again even if each time we get a bit more scared as the threats become more global). This is the one light we have to go by and trust that it will guide us through when the safer, simpler world we felt more at home in seems so lost.

I heard a bird sing in the dark of December

Amazing - almost miraculous - that I should receive David's latest Godspot the day after a remarkable Friends Meeting in Whitehaven. We had few reasons to be joyful. Our meeting is so sadly depleted by the deaths or departure for other reasons of dearly loved Friends that we have seriously considered closing our Meeting House. Our meeting was troubled by doubtful thoughts about Christmas, the cause of so many inflated hopes and so many disappointments, and many of us felt repelled by the idea that Jesus was born of a virgin, with its implication that to be conceived by a woman in the normal way is to be born in sin. Perhaps the only thing that held us together was the conviction that Jesus expresses more clearly and simply than anyone else the thought that we are all inadequate, we all need one another and let one another down, and need to forgive ourselves and other people.

After the meeting David Day and Anne Wilson, who were recently married at the ancient Friends Meeting House at Pardshaw, led us in singing the lovely round:-

'I heard a bird sing in the dark of December,

A magical song that is sweet to remember,

It's nearer to spring than it was in September,..

Somehow the simple connection of the song with the primitive instincts that have always caused people to celebrate the darkest time of the year helped us to understand why it was important to go on. And then David Wood's thoughts about the dark night of the soul arrived.

Peter Watson

INTERLUDE

The disciples were gathered round the holy one and he asked them a question. "When does the day begin?" One replied, "with the first sliver of light on the horizon?" No. Another said – "when the shadows begin to disappear and you can start to pick out details?" No A third – "when the first bird sings?" Wrong again. "When the sun comes up?" "No" said the holy one. "The day begins when you can see in every face you meet the face of God. Otherwise it is still night".

An April Fool

When my brother and I were quite young we took a morning cup of
tea to Mum and Dad in bed, working hard to keep our faces straight.
They couldn't believe their eyes at their amazing thoughtful boys
until no tea came out of the pot. " Da da de da da! April Fool!" April
1st is a day when you catch people out by leading them to think one
thing when the opposite is actually the case. The truth contradicts
expectations.

This year All Fools Day is Good Friday. Good Friday? It's the day
when Christians celebrate a crucifixion. And because this nation, as
all the nations in Europe, was built on the Christian view of life,
there are crucifixes everywhere. People even wear them round their
necks, in the ears. Christians celebrate failure, the failure of their
hero. Crucifixion means just that. He was a washout; in his lifetime a
flop. He made others feel a fool because he didn't deliver what they
expected. Nil return in their eyes, even though he healed people and
did miracles and got lots of followers. He went around saving others
but without a care for himself. You can't live like that so they made a
Fool out of him instead. 'That's what we think of your way of life'.
Oh yes, he went around believing in God but in the end it was as if
God was saying "The joke's on me folks!" Jesus got was coming to
him right between the eyes with that crown of thorns. Painful, but he
asked for it. Loved everyone so much that he was prepared to die for
them? You and me included? Rubbish!

The thing is, I keep on meeting people all over the place who are
very like Jesus. Just around the corner. At your elbow. You'll find
them in places across the way, down the street, all over West
Cumbria or wherever you happen to live. People always on the
lookout for number 2 or 3 or 4 but showing no concern for looking
after number 1. Pouring out their life's blood on what's obviously a
lost cause. When others are saying 'Why bother?' they bother. When
the world is saying 'What a fool wasting all that time and money and
effort, useless', they just keep on keeping on, through every hurt and
disappointment imaginable. It doesn't matter. Out of sheer love for
people.

I have met so many ordinary people wasting their lives caring for useless human beings wrecked by illness or evil or social disease. I think about them and it makes me weep at how beautiful they are. A waste? The love people give always makes new life after they have died. Always, though you may never see it. Seeds of love sown today for tomorrow. Only if a seed falls into the ground and dies does it bear fruit, ask any gardener. The good people do lives after them, the evil is buried with their bones.

So stop a minute and look at that figure on the cross. Look into that face and you will see your own. Your real self, even though such good love may be sunk very low under layers of make believe, of shame and sham. Christians believe that Jesus came to show us ourselves. We are all capable of allowing ourselves to be crucified for the sake of others when the chips are down. It's alright to appear a failure for the sake of love, to lay your life on the line for somebody else. The real fool is not Jesus, it is the one who refuses to accept this picture of himself or herself.

April Fool? Well, it's not the end of the story............

This story happens to be about a nun who made a real fool of herself but it could just as easily be about you. Elizabeth Pilenko joined a religious order in Russia. She was accused by some of neglecting the long traditions of the Church. In the early mornings she was at the market buying cheap food for the people she fed, bringing it back in a sack on her back. She was a familiar figure in the slum, in her poor black habit and her worn-out men's shoes.

In Paris she discovered Russian refugees who had contracted T.B. lying in a filthy hovel on the banks of the river Seine. With 10 francs, she bought a ruined chateau and opened a sanatorium. She became known as Mother Maria. Under her influence churches around Paris became real havens for the poor, served by the convent she founded. One even ran an employment exchange. When the second world war started, the convent became a refuge for Jews, and hundreds escaped through its work. After a month the Gestapo came.

63

Mother Maria was arrested and sent to the concentration camp at Ravensbruck. There she was known even to the guards 'as that wonderful Russian nun' and it is doubtful whether they had any intention of killing her.

She had been there two and a half years when a new block of buildings was erected in the camp, and the prisoners were told that these were to be hot baths. A day came when a few dozen prisoners from the women's quarters were lined up outside the buildings. One girl became hysterical. Mother Maria, who had not been selected, came up to her. "Don't be frightened", she said. "Look, I shall take your turn", and in line with the rest, she passed through the doors. It was Good Friday, 1945.

The Way, the Truth and the Life

There is a saying at the heart of Christian faith:- Jesus said "I am the Way, the Truth and the Life. No one can come to the Father except through me".

It is in St. John's Gospel, Chapter 14 verse 6. I frequently hear it said in Christian circles that this means that there is only one true faith and you cannot get to God in any way other than by being a Christian, explicitly and openly. There is only one Path. Christians have got the one True Light. So sorry, other believers, people of other faiths! You're not going to get there believing what you do. Come to Jesus for the real McCoy.

I do not believe that. On the face of what Jesus apparently said I suppose I ought to particularly when bishops go around making this saying a central plank of all they say and do and giving a clear and definitive impression: teaching it sounds like all other faiths are inferior. Jesus is the only one. Christians have got the best and one day everyone else will see that and come home.

But I believe there is another way of understanding this central saying, and for me the key is to appreciate the difference between 'Jesus' and 'Christ'. The writer of St.John's Gospel is not recording words Jesus actually spoke but is in fact writing a play, a drama with Jesus as the central character, interpreting what has been handed down, either written or spoken. For him 'Jesus' is the man on earth and 'Christ' is God's Word. God 'speaks' the Word within everyone. It is there in the beginning of every life, every life form. It is the Light in us all, in everything and nothing can ever put it out (the first chapter of St. John's Gospel says all this).

What I think St. John is trying to say is that no one can perceive, 'know', come to God (the Father, or Mother if you will!) unless they live the sort of life that Jesus lived. No one can get near except through the Jesus way of life. And he is also saying that the possibility of living that sort of life is in us all. That is the Christlife, the divine life, the Universal Spirit of all Being. The Word is made Flesh in us all. Now that I believe.

The Christlife is so obviously being lived out in the lives of many who do not acknowledge and will never acknowledge the name of Jesus because of their culture, religious and historical background. They live as Jesus lived and die as Jesus died, often sacrificing their own lives for the sake of many, out of what you can easily call 'divine' compassion. But that does not mean that others have to explicitly acknowledge 'Jesus is Lord' or even know about Jesus in order to be with God. Christians need to honour them and see them as spiritual equals, indeed bow the knee before their extraordinary lives. The wisdom writings of all the ages from all comers of the earth are full of the Christlife. We can share with other faiths equal to equal, not to dispute or deny or compete, nor to minimise the differences, but to be illuminated in our own tradition by them.

Jesus is the man for me. I have no doubt about that. He for me was God amongst us. And I will always want to point others in his direction and say, "look". Yes I want others to 'come to Jesus'.

In my early days I knew a family where there was a terrible tragedy. The boyfriend took the daughter out on his motorbike one night (no crash helmets then) and she was killed going round a bend too fast. The boyfriend came straight back to the girl's home and shut himself up in her bedroom, refusing to leave for more than two weeks. The mother of the family in all her desperate grief and without any recrimination just let him be there. His recklessness had killed her daughter. She looked after him every day until he eventually emerged. I remember telling her (rather pompously it sounds now) that she was living the life that Jesus lived. She didn't know what I was talking about, but in my language she was living with God in a way I knew nothing about.

The Sunlight is the People

Vocation? Calling? You don't see yourself as having one? Wrong. Everyone is called. Everyone. Not just special people with special jobs. One of the most desperate things I ever hear is church people saying about vicars 'Oh well, they're called' as if all the rest are not. Everyone has a calling in them, a longing to fulfil a particular heart's desire, to do what you feel you are for, when you feel perfectly synchronised in body, mind and spirit.

Calling has no need to have anything to do with worship of a God or being a holy person. But it has everything to do with the spirit of the universe coursing through human life. Calling is the spirit which animates the world (call it 'God' if you're that way inclined), it's all part of the new heaven on earth we are constantly called to make.

Sadly for many any sense of call can be smothered by the sort of lives they have to live. Yet it is there, inkling away inside like an insistent hidden voice. It may be high-profile - going to work with Aids victims in Zambia, Poland Aid; yes being a doctor, a teacher, a probation officer. Being an M.P. - they're not all in it for themselves

It is more likely to be a low-profile - growing roses, keeping pigeons, animal rescue, singing in choirs, painting pictures, volunteer in the Oxfam shop, befriending one elderly, lone person down the street, raising money for some good cause, being a mother at home. There is this man on the T.V. show, Britain has Talent. He is a lorry driver and at night delivers pizzas. He has always had a desire to sing in front of a large audience. He now has his chance and he is terrified, dumb struck, almost paralysed with fright. 'I'll go on there and dry up!' He is virtually pushed out onto the centre stage and his body language says it all, cowed, bowed. He can hardly answer basic questions. Then the music and he starts to sing. Within 2 minutes the whole audience is up on its feet, clapping, cheering. He is utterly bewildered. Someone comes up to him shortly afterwards and says – "How do you feel?" He simply replies, "Complete".

Whatever, it is something you feel fits you. You may not be able to live it with a large part of your life which requires you to earn money or stick where you are - but it is crucial to listen to our 'voice' and make some space for the 'call' to grow in. Mother Teresa (high-profile) describes herself as doing something beautiful for God. Whatever it is it will have a feel of doing something beautiful and true and right.

It has nothing to do with success or achievement, and it may look risky or unwise to the onlooker. It may feel like sticking your neck out. It has everything to do with love, loving what you do and with an unspoken sense of contributing to make the world a better, fairer, place with your tiny piece of the jigsaw. It can be anything.

I once heard an expert clockmaker on telly say "at the age of five I saw the insides of a watch and I knew at that moment what I was for".

Each living being, no matter how old, has something to do which is utterly important to him/her. And a calling may change as you complete what you set out to do or as life moves on. Calling is about change and being changed by what you choose to become involved in.

Everyone who seeks to follow a calling is a hero. It usually takes courage and persistence and may well lead to a whole series of failures. That's fine. The worst failure is always to sit back and do nothing to make it come true. True is beautiful. Small is beautiful. Just take one step, and if it seems good though wobbly, dangerous perhaps, take another.

Calling can grow out of our weaknesses - take the paraplegic games. A company of heroes. Bell, who was deaf, invented the telephone. It may be a gift you hesitate to use for fear you will attract attention and perhaps arouse scorn or envy.

The sunlight is the people. A high-profile leader may be the magnifying glass which sets the grass ablaze but the energy is the people. History knows no greater power than ordinary acts of courage. The sunlight is the people.

A man found an eagle's egg and put it in a hen's nest. The eagle hatched and grew up with the other chicks, scratting the earth for worms and insects, clucking, cackling just like the others.

One day a passing stranger saw it and said to the farmer "Hey, you've got an eagle there". "No" says the farmer "it's a chicken". The stranger put the eagle on his wrist and said "Fly" but the eagle hopped back down to peck along with the others. The stranger started to call each day bringing food proper to an eagle. After a few weeks he again took the bird on his wrist and said "Go on, fly". The bird stretched its great wings but again looking down hopped back to the yard. "There" said the farmer "I told you it was a chicken".

Next morning just at dawn the stranger returned. He took the bird on his wrist and led it a little way off. As the sun rose and tipped with morning gold the distant mountains he held the bird high and whispered, "Now, now, you're an eagle. Fly!" And reaching out its mighty wings it lifted up with effortless movement, circled into the morning and was away, soaring, soaring, doing what it was made for.

INTERLUDE

God can be realized through all paths.

All religions are true. The important thing is to reach the roof.

You can reach it by stone stairs or by bamboo steps or by rope. You can also climb by a bamboo pole.

Every religion has errors.

Everyone thinks that his watch alone gives the correct time. It is enough to have yearning for God.

It is enough to love Him and feel attracted to Him.

Don't you know that God is the inner guide? He sees the longing of our heart and the yearning of our soul.

Suppose a man had several sons. The older boys address him distinctly as 'Baba' or 'Papa' but the babies can at best call him 'Ha' or 'Pa'. Now will the father be angry with those who address him in this indistinct way? The father knows that they too are calling him, only they cannot pronounce his name well. All children are the same with their father.

Likewise, the devotees call on God alone, though by different names. They call on one Person only.

God is one, but His names are many. (Sri Ramakrishna)

<u>Silence and Stillness - The Hub of the Wheel</u>

Meet Action Ant. Ant was clinging to the rim of a mountain bike as it sped up hill and down dale. Bog, moorland, ruts and stones, spiky bits, great pools of mud - life was stinking rough, literally a vicious circle. Ant began to slither down one of the spokes towards the hub, and lo and behold!, life went round a little more slowly. After a bit Ant managed to come to rest on the central axle and found that here was total stillness, although the wheel was still spinning through the passing scene.

Now at the centre, Action Ant could rest and recollect itself and makes the vital discovery that unless the wheel was balanced in the still centre of the hub, it had no direction or power at all. It was useless. Ant also learned to move out to the rim, where the fast track was, and back, as it chose. Each person has a still centre and needs to go there. People need stillness. Unless you learn to be still you die. It is necessary to practise stopping and being still. There are a lot of people living on the rim all the time and they are dead on their feet. Sooner or later they grind to a halt. We are easily seduced into being over-active, brutally noisy, bristling with bustle, and forget how to be still. The centre is lost.

Unsatisfied longings are often just this - a longing to know how to be still. People are so dizzy that they have become afraid of stopping, so instead of silence within being welcomed as a friend, a warm and contented place, it is feared as an enemy, dark and dangerous.

Some native porters were being driven hard by their European employers along the jungle trails. On and on, they had to get there yesterday. Besides, the Europeans were afraid of what was hidden in the undergrowth. On the third morning the porters stopped and refused to go another step. "No!", they said, "we go no further at present. We have been travelling so fast we must now wait for our souls to catch up".

Imagine your life as a ship and you the captain. You're in charge on the bridge and on deck there is much to be seen and done. Below the waterline, however, well out of sight is the engine room and the engine is the driving force. This is the only part of the ship that was designed by the maker and delivered with it - all the rest was added after. Without giving the engine proper attention, the right fuel and constant maintenance, this ship is not going anywhere.

Listen to the Wisdom of the Ages:- 'Listen to your own heart in your own room and be still' - (Bible Psalm 4.)

'The path to all great things leads through stillness' - (Neitzche)

'God is everywhere, even on Broadway, but we can only hear His voice in silence' -(Ernesto Cardinal)

'Be still and know who God is' - (Bible Psalm 46)

'Just as the petals of a water lily uncurl when the sun shines, so closed parts of people unfold when they are silent' - (Joyce Huggett)

You will find love deep within, but you have to take time to stop and listen.

P.S. Perhaps I should have left this page blank so that you could just rest and be still rather than flick on through.

EXPANDING HORIZONS

<u>A New Age - scary</u>

Here is my creed, what I believe. I believe in the dawn of a new age. We are in the darkness before that dawn and we are speeding towards it. We are giving birth, that's what we are doing and it's a messy business. Birth isn't all joy and light, sanitary loveliness and no pain. It can be slick and quick yet often it is drawn out, a sometimes ugly, sometimes beautiful gripe. It may be chaos in the back of a taxi or suddenly up there in a Boeing 747 - you sometimes wish it wasn't happening but you can't stop what has started. The birth of a new age is the same.

Old Moores with their almanacs, astrologers, geophysicists and apologists, and other wise men say there is plenty of evidence that every 2000 years or so there is a huge shift in human history and attitude.

In the process of giving birth a lot of the old life has to be left behind, some of it with regret ("when" say the new mother and father "did we ever have time before"?). The birth of a new age means the death of an old age. The human race is moving house and you have to decide what to take with you and what to leave behind. There will be disagreements and sometimes a wrong decision is made.

We are scared of change, terrified of massive change. Fear of the unknown makes us run around like headless chickens bumping into each other, panic dressed up as greed, grabbing hold of lifelines that aren't really lifelines at all. It can look like death, doom and destruction and nothing else, the Four Horsemen have arrived.

You must know the story of the man who fell over a precipice and managed to clutch a shrub on the way down. "Oh my God" he yelled "HELP". And he heard a voice sounding remarkably like what people would think God's voice would sound like if God had a voice – "Do you really want my help?" "Course I do". "Very well then" the voice said "do exactly as I say if you want to be safe". "Yes, yes, hurry" says the man. God: "Let go". A long pause, then the man, "Is there anybody else there?"

74

I believe in this new age that we are being called, yes called, by the driving energy of Life and Universe to enter into the next stage of development as humankind. What we shall be changed into from what we are we do not know, but we are being led forward into a new state of consciousness, a higher life. Awareness is central, we shall become ever more and more aware of every mortal thing, every living being. Already year by year we are more global, cosmic in thought, word and deed - the 85 year old gran jets regularly to Australia to see her son and family, or even does a parachute jump. Education may begin at your local primary school but it zooms straightway out of the classroom on the internet across the world.

Have you heard of compassion fatigue? Do you suffer from it like I do from time to time? You have weighed it all up. You have given as generously as you think you can to all the charitable appeals that come at us with unrelenting regularity, and then the very next day, another drops through the letterbox, squares in on your television eye. You feel worn out with it, it's too much. But do you not see, such fatigue is a good sign, it is marvellous, not an ill. We are more open in our hearts and minds to other's needs than ever we were. Cosmic kids, cosmic pensioners -brilliant.

I believe Jesus is the best model for living and dying and is already in high fashion. Not as the Christ in majesty of cloister and holy place but Jesus the donkey man, way out, unsung and unnamed, on the garbage tip of piled up, left-behind humanity. The multitude of purposeful men and women who choose to 'waste' their lives by waiting at roadside and bedside with those who have no choice but to wait, often helplessly, is a constant hymn of praise across the hills and valleys of our world. A bright song of hope.

I believe that the world's religions must leave behind their fossilized state and come together in a unity which will celebrate similarities and rejoice in each other's differences. I believe that this is not only the best hope but the last hope to save civilisation from the savageries of the competitive spirit which have no place in a new age. We have nothing to lose but our fear. Of each other.

INTERLUDE

A Hindu picture of God:-

I do dimly perceive that whilst everything around me is ever changing, ever dying, there is underlying all that change, a living power that is changeless, that holds all together, that creates, dissolves and recreates. That informing power or spirit is God. And since nothing else that I see merely through the senses can or will persist, He alone is.

And is this power benevolent or malevolent? I see it as purely benevolent. For I can see that in the midst of death life persists, in the midst of untruth truth persists, in the midst of darkness light persists. Hence I gather that God is Life, Truth, Light. He is Love. He is the Supreme Good.

(Mahatma Gandhi 1869 to 1945, when he was assassinated by one who couldn't bear the thought of change).

On the way out?

Into a new school year and our amazing young. Kevin's been staying with his gregarious friend, Blackberry. Blackberry is unnerving. He (it) can tell me how to drive from our front door to John O'Groats never having been asked the question before; how to fly to L.A.; how many nautical miles it is from Maryport across the Solway to Kirkcudbright; that my nearest Tandoori is 250 yards away (now I could have told him that!) He checks my spelling at Scrabble, tells me the latest cricket scores, talks to someone he has never met in Cyprus, and checks 25 e-mails from work for Kevin before breakfast, though work is 7 hours flying time away. Blackberry goes everywhere with Kevin, and often just sits at the table with us or in the chair. I suspect he gives Kevin sore thumbs and oh! he certainly can't cut toe nails. Richard has the same friend.

Me, I'm a Raspberry. I'm dazzled by Blackberry's potential. Indeed Kevin's Blackberry is already getting out of date as bigger and juicier ones grow on the telecommunications vine. His reach is so vast it scares me, but that's only my ignorance in an expanding universe I know nothing about. I can't catch up even if I wanted to, which I don't. "It's just your age, love", someone said to me and that's a long time ago. My Age, and I'm not just speaking for myself, is passing away (very biblical that!) Out of my grasp. Too fast, too clever for me.

There are lots of Blackberries about, multiplying every day, they belong to the future, and to the young. One guy who is normally rather gloom and doom, was hugely cheered recently at a graduation ceremony by the brightness and optimism of the young. They are vastly different from me and my times; less likely to turn up to things, they are constantly connected and communicate differently. They value open and honest communication (their activity on the web is 'a wonder to behold', and they mistrust institutions and politicians). Civic minded, have little interest in race, gender or sex orientation: yes to flexible working, and getting a proper work/life -balance, bored by routine; success-driven, anti-commitment, environmental, entrepreneurial, goal-orientated - etc!!

I do not understand: I'm a bit alarmed. But it's me who is on the way out, not them, they are mainstream. It is however, as it always has been for me, God's world. God far ahead of us in the world, as usual. And Blackberry is only one unfolding glimmer of the Energy that propels, compels the universe about which we all know so very little. We have to trust, especially we have to trust our young. They are <u>our</u> young. And your work, my work while I live, is to remain content with and faithful to my raspberryness, and witness to the young that the wisdom of the ages (always addressed as 'she' in the bible, now there's a thing) has other flavours to be discovered, sometimes sweeter, if slower, than the Blackberry of speed and progress; and without which any progress, any change will be at the least tasteless and at the worst only worth spitting out. In the meantime be content to be amazed at so many glorious young.

<u>Fragile</u>

We are fragile. Very, very fragile. All the fitness gymnasia in the world cannot do anything about that. Let's remind ourselves who and what we are, how we are made. How am I made?

I am a skeleton, everything hangs on that, is built up from it. It is my frame. I am lungs, I breathe, I have a respiratory system which constantly regenerates me. I am stomach, gut, alimentary canal, a digestive system which feeds me. And I am blood, a circulatory system which purifies and revitalises the body. This inter-balance of systems is basic me. Damage any one part and I soon experience how fragile I am, when one goes down all are affected.

The Earth is exactly the same. It is not a dull, inanimate clod, like a ball of clay we can throw around, shape and reshape as we may. Like us it is a living system, made in exactly the same way. It has a skeleton-rocks, its core, tectonic plates, mountain ranges which frame everything else. The Earth breathes just as we breathe, its lungs are plants, trees, all vegetation constantly renewing the entire atmosphere. It has a digestive system, the soil. The Earth is forever munching - everything is taken in, absorbed, broken down and recycled. The Earth's lifeblood is its oceans and waterways.

Mother. Mother Earth lives and we have grown out from her in exactly the same way. She has given us what she has.   What's more, the Earth maintains an average body temperature and the salinity of the ocean within certain limits. Beyond those limits life would not exist. Exactly with us. Our body temperature range is marvellously close - 98.4 to 100+. Below that we clog up, by 105 we are dead.

That elite company of people, astronauts, trained to the highest degree technically, physically, mentally, all say the same. As they cruise space, watching the Earth rise, as they watch the moon or sun rise, they have been filled with awe at the fragility of Earth. And their lives have been changed.

We are fearfully and wonderfully made. The balance of it all is so delicate. The story of our evolution to this point is an amazing focusing down through billions of years to a very narrow opening where life became possible and then on again to the point where human life became possible. Outside those limits none of it would have happened. Where are we? Those who know and measure tell us that it has taken 5 billion years to develop our solar system - a measure of time impossible to grasp. But if we say that 5 billion years = 1 year, then 8 months were taken up in the development of the atmosphere and biosphere from gaseous beginnings. It then took 4 months for higher life forms to develop. The measure of the development of the human consciousness is simply one day at the end of all this. Just pause for a moment.

Of that one day 23 and a half hours is prehistory. The last 30 minutes is all we know of the great civilisations and their histories, and the last few minutes of this day is the age of industrial revolution, science and technology, and our present age.

What is the difference between a 'house' and a 'home'? A house is a building with 4 walls and some rooms. You put it up, roof it, plaster and decorate it and fill it with furniture. You come and go. A home is a place that feels lived in, cared for, shelters people and families who depend on each other and look out for each other.

It's a treasured, nurturing, comforting place with a life of its own. Some people live in houses, some live in homes.

The Earth is our home and it is fragile.   For centuries (during this last half hour) we have been exploiting, bullying, plundering, beating it, treating it as if it were an inanimate object, not a tender, subtle life-form. The Earth is hurt, it is bleeding, it is wounded. The Earth is our home and it is fragile. We have been turning our home into a house.

Humankind is not the pinnacle of creation. The Earth was not made just for us, we grew out of the Earth, we are made for each other. We have evolved as the only conscious life-form, we have been given the gift of thinking, reflecting, imagining.   We are if you like the Earth's eye by which it learns to see itself, the Earth's Consciousness. The Earth's Mind.

Someone said 'We are a star's way of knowing about the stars'. This is our function, our place. We all know what happens if we go on mindlessly abusing our bodies, year after year. Eventually the body just packs in. Gives up and dies.

Perhaps at the end of this half hour we are starting to grow out of adolescence as humankind and come of age in starting to recognise how everything is interrelated, mixed together in a cosmic soup called Energy. Or Love. The life of science and the life of the spirit are converging at last to share in exploring what all acknowledge is our profound and expanding Mystery (to call this mystery God is to give it far too small a name).

What we have to learn is that our existing money systems which depend on extracting without putting back, of maximising profit regardless of consequence, if they continue, will kill off Mother Earth. Before long. It means profound changes in the way we trade and view life on our planet which will mean some sacrifice and discomfort and new levels of awareness and sensitivity - we shall have to know more what it is like to carry one another's burdens. It's a huge problem but it is not somebody else's problem.

That lovely tough 20th century prophet and saint of West Cumbria, Alan Ecclestone has words to guide us. To pray, he says, is to refuse to be disengaged with the world's ills, even if they make you feel insignificant and helpless. Suffering the problem, living with it, changes it.

So often a very sick person has been brought back to health because someone stayed with them, holding their hand, wiping their brow, helplessly, not quite knowing what to do, talking to them, just being there. 'Conscious to conscious'. One reason why the Church has become disgraced in the public eye is that many who claimed to be Church did not, in this way, pray. That can still often enough be true, yet I think this is changing.

Mother Earth is fragile . We are fragile. Hang in - this is the way to live in the 21st century.

INTERLUDE

To get real here is a picture of evolution as presented in a one-year cycle.

1st January:	The Big Bang
7th February:	The Milky Way is born

14th August:	The Earth is born
4th September:	First life on the Earth

15th December:	The Cambrian explosion
25th December:	The dinosaurs appear
30th December:	Extinction of the dinosaurs

31st December

19.00.00: First human ancestors
23.58.00: First humans
23.59.30: Age of Agriculture
23.59.47: The pyramids
23.59.58: Jesus Christ is born
23.59.59: Galileo is born
24.00.00: Today

Trees

'Trees for me have always been the most convincing of preachers. I admire them when they stand in copses, in woods or plantations. But most of all, I admire them when they stand alone. They are solitary. Not like hermits, who out of some weakness creep away on their own, but like great, lonely people such as Beethoven and Nietzsche. In their crowns the world whispers, and their roots rest in the eternal; they do not lose themselves in eternity but strive with all their strength towards one end: to fulfil the law within them, to build their own shape, to become themselves. Nothing is more holy, nothing more exemplary, than a beautiful strong tree.

When a tree is felled and its naked wound is exposed to the sun: then you can read in the pale disc of its stump the history of its life: in the growth rings are written all suffering, all illnesses; all joy and times of health; lean years and fat years; attacks withstood, storms survived. And every country child knows that the finest wood has the narrowest rings, that the most resilient and noble trees grow high up in the mountains where danger is ever present.

Trees are shrines. He who knows how to speak with them, who knows how to listen to them, experiences truth. They preach no catechism or recipe, they preach the original law of life.

A tree speaks: within me is hidden a kernel, a spark, a thought; I am life from eternal life. The eternal mother has made me unique: my shape, the web of my branches, unique; the smallest play of leaves in my crown, the tiniest scar on my bark, unique. My role is to show and give shape to the unique and the eternal.

A tree speaks: my strength is trust. I know nothing of my forbears, I know nothing of the thousands of baby trees which spring from me each year. I live the secret of my seed to the end, nothing else concerns me. I trust that God is within me. I trust that my task is holy. Out of this trust I have life.

When we are sad and life seems too hard to bear, then a tree can speak to us: Be still! Be still! Look at me! Life is not easy, life is not difficult. Those are childish thoughts. Let God speak in you, and those thoughts will be stilled. You are fearful, because your path is taking you away from your mother and your home. But every step and every day leads you afresh towards your mother. Home is not here or there. Home is within you, or nowhere.

A restlessness grips my heart when I hear trees whispering in the evening breeze. But listen quietly for a little longer, and that restlessness begins to make sense. It is not the yearning to escape from suffering, as you first thought. It is the yearning for home, for the memory of the mother, for the parable of life. She leads us home. Every path leads home, every step is birth, every step is death, every grave is Mother.

So whispers the tree in the evening, when we are fearful of our own childish thoughts. Trees think long thoughts, breath slow breaths, because their lives are longer than ours. They are wiser than us, as long as we fail to hear them. But when we have learnt how to listen to trees, then the brevity and speed and childish haste of our thoughts will gain a new sense of joy. He who has learnt to listen to trees, stops longing to be a tree. He longs for nothing more than to be who he is. That is home. That is happiness'.

(Herman Hesse - translated by Polly Clarke)

Love expands, or dies

As the Light in the sky expands with the year, let's have a slice of what's really Real. Do you know that the Vatican has an observatory to explore the heavens and the universe complete with a director/cosmologist? And what's that got to do with being a parent, or God for that matter? Let's start with parents because that is easier.

If you are seeking to be a truly loving parent to your children, they will show you ever deeper ways of how you may love them. You learn to evolve as a human being, with them, because of them. Sometimes that is sheer joy, delight that knows no bounds. Sometimes it is hard graft as you learn when to speak or shut up, when to act or do nothing. And sometimes it is one of the most deeply painful experiences of being alive, when children seem to turn against and betray all you thought you stood for, everything you have tried to show them of love. There are also sheer terrible mistakes - the times, the many times, when they are hurting real bad and you can do nothing except stand by full of helpless love.

And it's different with each child, all your growing pains with them are unique. Your love, if you can manage to stay the course, is never static, it is expanding all the time. Your heart ,which is simultaneously happy/satisfied/glad/sad/broken/torn apart/ grows larger and larger. It is the story of Life.

If in yourself you are stuck with one model of love that never changes, a given:- "I know it all in advance, the trouble is the little 'b----s' just won't 'b----y' well listen and do as I say" - then you are dead though you may actually live into an unripe old age. The odds are our children will turn out very differently from what we want them to be: that terrible story: two mothers meet, one says to the other "How old are your children now?" The other replies "The doctor is 5 and the ballet dancer is 3".

The cosmologist, with constantly developing equipment and advanced mathematics/physics offers this:- 'Will the universe ever end? Can we rely on it to continue on and on? The most recent measurements of the velocities of recession of very distant objects in the universe, supernovae, which can serve as standard 'light beacons' at distances of about 10 to 12 billion light years from us, indicate that the universe is not only still expanding but that it is accelerating in its expansion and will, unless we discover a braking mechanism, expand forever - an empirically infinite universe'.

Our understanding of God needs to expand likewise. God is not a master architect with a vast blueprint laid out on a drawing board. God is not the universe, but God is working with the evolutions of the universe. It is not all cut and dried, there are <u>chance</u> elements all through these evolutions, and in these evolutions there are inevitable necessary elements. One necessity is that an accelerating universe will be dead.: there will be no energy (you could say that God is forever taking chances which is what love is all about). There is also huge <u>creative power</u> surging through it all. The universe has a vitality of its own, like a child with its unique passion for life, and 'the universe has the ability to respond to words of endearment and encouragement'. God, if you like, is a prompt. 'Words that give life are richer than commands or information' as any parent eventually knows. Our picture of God needs to expand to see God as going with the flow like any constant lover rather than as a master designer, imposing his will.

(My debt here is to George Coyne, director of the Vatican observatory).

<u>Sex - yes please!</u>

Yes...Yes!....YES! Yes to Sex! I love the story about the teacher who started to talk to the class about sex, morality and happiness. "At times when we are tempted we need to ask ourselves just one question - is an hour of pleasure worth a lifetime of regret?" She went on a bit and then asked if there were any questions. One student immediately raised his hand, "Please miss, can you tell us how you make it last an hour?"

That's not quite what I meant though. Yes to sex. Yes in sex means Yes to God. Even if you don't know it. Even if you never know it (which is a pity). Sex is the basic root, the start of it all. Isn't it? Don't tell me it isn't, my little seedlings, or else how did you arrive? Not still into storks and gooseberry bushes are you? We are all sexual beings and sometimes we need to be reminded. Sometimes there is so much sex going on all around - kissy-kiss and humpy-hump -that we can feel, or want to feel, shut off from it as if it is not part of us. It is everywhere. It sometimes feels like a dance of the dervishes going on 'out there', it all seems so casual and profligate for many. A good night out is not complete without sex with a stranger - sad but real world, for many.

But I have to ask, is this howling after one another any worse than a sexual abstinence which is as dry as old autumn leaves, a sort of hands-off-me-I'm-human approach to life and love and partnership? Many partnerships have disintegrated into autumn leaves. The one is a deluge, an uncontained flood, the other bleak famine, desert landscape. Both kill life.

Back to basics however is to recall above all that God and Sex go together from the beginning. God is in there, right in there, enjoined, enfleshed, inseparable, man into woman, woman enfolding man. Blood of my blood, bone of my bone. To practice one and deny the other is finally to desecrate all human value. We are each a temple. The saint was approached for advice by a young man overwhelmed by desire for a woman he found gorgeous. "Just make sure" the saint said "that you don't pee on the altar".

Sexual desire is an in-flesh longing which lasts in one way or another for the whole of a life's journey. It is the impulse to throw oneself into love, an impulse implanted in the seed, in God, to reach out passionately to that which is beyond speech and imagination - ultimate truth and beauty; to have a home in a world where it feels as if you will not be allowed to rest anywhere safely for long (here we have no abiding city).

True prayer is like sex. True sex is like prayer, in-flesh together. Both are about paying attention to the other, a yearning to communicate. Each, sex and prayer, offers the promise of personal fulfilment which can only be found not in oneself but in and through another. Every sexual climax is a way of dying, a way of yearning to disappear into another dimension. The God-given facts of life are that we can only discover Life and Truth about life through others.

Let it be known that one reason why the young find the life of the Church so arid is that it often seems so sexless, no flesh on the bone. Let it also be said that one reason why the young find sex so mechanical, a short sharp gasp, is that they are not able to bring it any spiritual life.

Passion without commitment is reckless waste. This coming in-flesh together needs profound humility. The Chief Rabbi, Jonathan Sacks describes humility. He says, "The creed of our age - If you've got it, flaunt it – doesn't give humility much of a chance; but that doesn't mean it is out of date". However, he says, humility does not mean undervaluing yourself (I'm ever so 'umble). What it does mean is valuing others. It means treating the other (whoever it is, whenever it is) as if they were the most important person in the world. "It became clear to me when I met this person", he said "that they believed in me more than I believed in myself." This is the heart of sex. It is the heart of God.

'Sexual desire is also to be seen as a gift from God which means it is charged with a character described as holy, an awesome and often explosive thing. Misused it can blast and wither….. baulked and perverted it can poison relationships…..Gifts of such dangerous power can neither be ignored not handed back……To lose sight of the person, to ignore the claims of personal responsibility, the price of such neglect and indifference is ultimately Auschwitz'. (Alan Ecclestone)

INTERLUDE

Ah, when shall I get to gaze upon
the unique One to whom no other compares.
With mind melting, melting,
growing more and more tender -
standing, sitting, lying, rising,
laughing, weeping, serving, praising -
when shall I dancing do all these things?
With hair bristling, bristling,
when am I going to gaze upon His holy form,
which gleams like the sunset,
and enter union with Him?
When shall I be united with my uncut Gem?

(The Soul in Love Transformed - Tiruvacakan - a Tamil
saint)

Rape

Imogen, age 4, every night at her beloved watersport bath time, is a jazz.
What a hoot that child is. Then there's Jake, her brother, forever
grimeing in from the latest football match: is there any mud left on the
pitch you may wonder. Whatever, the day washes off and they emerge
pink and wholesome. Lucky them. 'In Northern Kenya rainy seasons
are disappearing. Nomads who have coped for generations with a
difficult climate by moving their herds from waterhole to waterhole,
while their roaming gives the terrain time to recover, can no longer do
so. Not only their livelihood but also their culture and way of life are
being destroyed'.

Meanwhile all our politicians continue to play dodgems with us. If you
want to keep power or win power to pursue political dreams, you
constantly have to stroke the electorate. Woo us – 'it's not all that bad,
it'll get better' stuff. Well it won't, it's not true any more, and the issue

is climate change. Repeat, Climate Change, the persistent rape of our Mother Earth. If you rape someone continually they will die sooner or later. Or if not quite that the someone you know will be entirely changed, permanently damaged. Earth is a Someone. The biggest Someone we know. Earth lives, breathes and has its being.

Don't associate rape with me, you will say. But we have to. Most of us in our society are rapists, despoiling, directly or indirectly the world on which we live. It's all very well talking about changing light bulbs, recycling, using bathwater to water the garden, hitting the gas- guzzlers with punitive taxes (including low-cost air travel? ouch!) It will do a wee bit, we all have to do our bit, but it's piddle-mee-ree. The nasty unelectable political word is 'sacrifice'. But that is what doing our bit for most of us now really means. It means learning to do with less ourselves, in some cases doing without what we have become accustomed to having, so that others may have a little. May regain their dignity, just live, survive. It is virtually certain amongst other things to mean our paying out more in tax. Less wealth for ourselves (less instant gratification, here and now stuff, must have it............., less credit).

There is little time left. It is now a life and death issue. Either we change, make sacrifices to our expected standard of living or people die. (Not a happy political slogan). It's already been happening for decades and we have gone on blithely as if it didn't matter. Ultimately this is a spiritual issue (a God issue if you will). Am I my brother's keeper or am I not? How we look upon the rest of the human race, our brothers and sisters whom we know or do not know, is fundamentally a spiritual matter. If we say "I am not" we shall destroy ourselves.

So fellow-rapists, what are we going to do?

In the meantime a prayer that any person of faith, or any religion can use:-

> "May we choose to cherish the earth and the oceans. May we explore and discover the wisdom of restraint. May there grow in each of us an ever deeper desire for the common good", (with thanks to Jim Cotter)

Go on, boggle

I know so little. I am staggered by how little. As one ancient said "I know more and more about less and less". Here I am after quite a long life, I turn a page and bingo, a completely new world of dazzling complexity, layer upon layer. For example we men and women are exceedingly clever the way we now put things together. The 'simple' mobile phone, it seems such a complex process to get the text on screen from my daughter in Dubai, I can't even get hold of that. The new shuttle, Discovery, is 'an airplane' with 2 million working parts, it contains 300 miles of wiring and travels more than 25 times the speed of sound. Wow!

And so the unfolding goes on, page after page. I waggle my fingers and am amazed at the complexity of structure which makes such a gesture possible - there are nails that grow, joints bend, blood flows, skin flourishes and as I bend my elbow a vast motorway of messages zips to and fro to my brain. During the middle stages of pregnancy trillions of nerve endings form in the unborn foetus. Trillions! As one of the poets of the bible writes in a psalm 'I am fearfully and wonderfully made. Such knowledge is too wonderful for me, so high that I cannot reach it'.

Turn yet another page, behind what humankind make and do and are, and we discover that there are 98,000 species of flies, 112,000 butterflies and a vast 290,000 species of beetle. (J.S. Haldane, a great scientist said that it looked as if the Creator has 'an inordinate fondness for beetles').

And this is just life before death. What about life beyond death? I was sitting in the crematorium the other day alongside the funeral of a good friend, John, when I had this image which in all my years I had never had before; 'the consciousness' contained in the body and is dead at death, is at death like a rocket taking off. It zooms up out of our known atmosphere of living on earth, like a rocket, dropping lots of body bits as it goes until it is much smaller in an absolutely new dimension (weightlessness); almost instantaneously transformed. Resurrection. We know nothing about life beyond death, except that Christians believe in resurrection. They will say that Jesus came to show us, all of us, not only how to live now but what to look forward to beyond death. Resurrection, Jesus is showing us, is universal, not just for the favoured faithful few; perhaps it is built into our genes, there for everybody. All that this life is about is like the rocket, preparing to take-off. Extraordinary detail, a million, trillion parts ready for takeoff. It's a beginning for the next part of the journey. Just because we don't know anything about it doesn't mean it's not there. And Jesus is saying to the world, don't let your ignorance make you afraid.

A barometer by which we can start to believe in resurrection is physics. What some physicists are thinking is that the whole driving force of the universe behind and beyond atoms and molecules, protons and electrons and neutrons, all the minute paraphernalia that makes the world go round, is consciousness. Our consciousness is there, in us, to be moved, elevated, shaped into different forms of being. Being continues, travels on, expands as we die, and each of us, individually, uniquely, is caught up in it and contributes to it.

These speculations do not contradict all that science knows about the world; rather it grows out of what is known as quantum physics and the current state of mathematics. You might not like the language but listen to this:- a personal life is an information-processing system and thoughts and feelings might ultimately be downloaded into what might be called clouds of spiritual consciousness into which we are transformed. In these nothing will be lost but all that has been experienced - the good at least - will be retained and we shall be open to vast new discoveries and meetings with other intelligences: we may come to see 'our own lives in the wider context of the total history of the universe. We might also come to know the lives and experiences of many other persons, and so have an experience far wider and richer than has been possible on earth'. (Keith Ward - regius professor of divinity, University of Oxford).

The internet and the worldwide web are just a glimmer here and now, of what such an expansion might be, a further preparation for the life the other side of death. Our universe could be one of many universes, this is an intelligible possibility. Here's a new word -maybe we live in a system called a 'multiverse', with the idea that there are parallel universes and we could move into them.

Of course we can't grasp it. It does not mean it's not there. When Columbus sailed off many thought there was nothing there. Flying? A submarine submerged for many months at a time? Landing on the moon? Going to Mars? - all poppycock. Resurrection, the Christian faith says, is a real dimension for everybody. Modern science is starting to say the same and this is what it may be like. Bon voyage, John!

91

Just remember - Jesus was a Jew

I grew up amongst Jews. Many were my friends at school - Simons, Praeger, Wolperwitz, Goldberg, Smidman - great guys. What we Gentile schoolboys really envied was that the Sabbath for Jews began at sunset on a Friday evening until sunset on Saturday and as the autumn and winter drew on, Jewish friends went home earlier and earlier as the sun set, because many Jewish families observed Sabbath very strictly, until eventually they seemed to have the whole afternoon off. Religion seemed quite a good thing.

So picture the scene. It's the Victoria Theatre, Salford, and a dark Saturday evening, the end of the Sabbath day. The theatre is packed with Jewish men and women of all descriptions: we are about the only Gentiles there. And as ever when Jewish people get together socially, it's like a street market. The noise is tremendous, people shouting across the theatre to one another, leaning over the balcony, calling down, waving across. Total hubbub. Fantastic.

And the occasion, a Night with David Kossoff, the great Jewish one-man show. For two hours or more he holds us spellbound with his story-spinning, and Jews love stories against themselves. Here is the only one I remember from that night:-

The Yiddisha Mamma is sitting at home. Her modern son has arrived home from the States with his new wife, a startling heavy blonde. Mother has not seen him for a long time, this is a flying visit. Eventually the young woman goes off to bed leaving mother and son to talk.
Mamma: "Tell me Hymie, is she Jewish?"
Hymie: "Ah well you know Ma, times have changed, you gotta go with the flow Ma, things aren't the same any more".(Pause)
Mamma: "Tell me Hymie, do you still keep the Sabbath?"
Hymie: "Ah well you know Ma, times have changed, you gotta go with the flow, things aren't what they used to be". (LONG, LONG PAUSE)
Mamma: "Tell me Hymie, are you still circumcised?"

A great contemporary storyteller about Jews is Rabbi Lionel Blue who broadcasts and writes regularly for the Catholic weekly 'The Tablet'. No matter what the topic, there is always a story. He tells how once as a young rabbi he was preaching with great passion and all the while an old man in the front snored away. Afterwards Rabbi Blue remonstrated with him sadly,

"You didn't hear a word I said". "Rabbi, Rabbi", the man replied, "don't take on so, I don't need to listen to you because I trust you so much".

I am a good mimic and when I was young one of the ways I could make people like me was to tell stories in the appropriate accent - Irish jokes about the Irish, Jewish jokes about the Jews, etc. Eventually I slowly realised that the only people who should tell such stories were the people themselves, Irish for Irish, Jew for Jew, because for me to do it was a put down. I was typecasting, stereotyping, it was laughing at them instead of with them, scapegoating them for our own stupidities.

The Jews so easily get a bad press. They are down the ages the classic people to run out of town. What is happening in Israel/Palestine is appalling, despicable beyond words and as a consequence anti-Semitism is on the rise. There are those who even say the Jews deserved The Holocaust. What it is very important to recognise is that within Jewry is Zionism and fanatical Zionism. Zionism is the drive to have a Jewish homeland in the Middle East. Fanatical, right-wing heavily political Zionism is the thirst to have this at any cost. There are many Jews who are Zionist, who want a homeland, but not at the cost of the vicious persecution, the cutting back and cutting down of Arab neighbours which we witness in the daily news. Many, many Jews, secular and religious, are greatly disturbed at the human cost of implementing Zionism. We can thoroughly and decently oppose the government policy of Israel without becoming Jew-haters: there is no justification for the vilification of all Jews. It is not that if we are pro-Arab we are anti-Jew, it is that basic human decencies and human rights are being deliberately ignored. In Israel/Palestine there are many deep cross-national friendships and on both sides strong movements working for solutions through dialogue and non-violent means.

The Jews have always known how to laugh at themselves so let Jewish humour have the last word:- A passing ship sees a white flag flying on a desert island and investigates to discover a Jew who has been shipwrecked there for 10 years. The rescuing officer notices two huts built on the two hills of the island, the one beautifully constructed, the other a ramshackle. "The beautiful one" explains the Jew, "is the synagogue I have prayed in all these years". All fall silent in respect. "So the other one must be your home" says the officer, indicating the ramshackle one. "Oh no!" is the reply, "that's the synagogue I wouldn't be seen dead in", (source Lionel Blue).

<u>Assisted dying</u>

Here tread very gently for it is holy ground. Before you pass
comment walk 2 miles in the other person's shoes. This is about
'assisted dying'. The Voluntary Euthanasia Society has changed its
name to 'Dignity in Dying', and there are truly agonised voices
around of those who, faced with intolerable suffering, seek to end
their own lives with personal dignity - before the worst fears and
onslaughts. To remain in control, in charge. Now, they say, when
we have more liberty in choosing how to live longer, we need to be
more free to die. There are things to commend it. Also it seems in
countries where it is already practised legally, chasms can open in
front of those who seek it. A principal difficulty can be that instead
of it being a 'last resort' it can all too easily become a 'first resort'
when faced with hard suffering.

On the other side is palliative medicine and the Hospice at
Home movement with its offer of pain-free dying in virtually
all situations.

Death is an ordinary rite of passage for us all however it arrives and
it has often been seen as part of the faith-journey through life. That
does not make it less hard. Perhaps what it comes down to is
choosing between on the one hand logic and reason and staying in
charge (assisted dying), and on the other faith and mystery and
handing over: here the queen of logic and rational calculation and
scientific method does not necessarily hold sway. Here's one story
of faith.

My good friend Peter, bright and strong in his late 50s', profoundly
Christian, has terminal cancer. Asbestos. The inevitable panics,
fears, desperate alarms and the gradual diminishing of powers.
Such suffering seems senseless, he says, and you yearn for a speedy
release when the time comes, whether for yourself or the one whose
bedside you sit at. And yet. There can be a 'gift' in it, he says, no
matter how deeply buried; a gift to the dying one and to those
around them. He says quite simply that his mother had senile
dementia and over several years the person that he and his sister

knew just disappeared. A long bereavement it was. Yet. As the dementia increased his mother's inhibitions of criticism and remoteness all fell away and she became the most abundantly loving person. Throughout his life he had questioned whether he was ever really loved and wanted as a child. All these doubts were 'washed away' by the obvious depth of her love. Coming out of her dementia, her lostness, he says, it was the greatest gift he had ever been given, a grace indeed. Others who cared for her in her home and later were similarly affected by her loving change.

Had his mother stepped in to end her life at an earlier stage in her illness to prevent herself from becoming 'degrading', it would have robbed 'all of us around her' of something infinitely precious reaching into life from beyond death.

You are a temple

How about a Cathedral where there is no mention of God? No God labels, no 'This is none other than the House of....' No explicit reference. And maybe this is not your idea of a Cathedral at all. No resemblance to Canterbury or Carlisle, Coventry or Cologne Cathedrals, Notre Dame, St. Peter's, Rome. Just a converted factory. Yet Cathedral it certainly is. I'm talking of course about Tate Modern, in London. When I went I found it stunning. It knocked me sideways. It is huge. It has cathedral dimensions and there are things in it that take your breath away - with beauty, shock, amazement, disbelief. For me, not infrequently, an 'ah yes' or an 'oh, wow'.

It is a Cathedral, there is no question, a Cathedral of the Human Spirit which is what older Cathedrals are anyway. I don't know how you are with modern art, I have never really got on with Picasso for example, with an eye here and an arm there, faces the wrong way round for me. Perhaps, for you, art should always be photographic, a picture you can instantly recognise (even better with a gilt frame round it?) And there's stuff in Tate Modern that should not, in my view, be there because it seems insincere; there's too much ego; look-at-me-doing-this in it.

Blowing a personal foghorn. Trashy. But I feel the same about Cathedrals in general - there's a lot of trash that shouldn't be there, monuments to a vain heart and personal glory, and a host, definitely not heavenly, of artistic rubbish.

But you can turn many corners at Tate Modern and be stopped in your tracks. What's this? What's it supposed to be, to represent, to say? You don't have to understand it to be rooted to the spot. You can sense something real and true coming through from it though you might not recognise what it is. Or might not want to recognise. There is a whole variety of images, assemblies, collages, confronting us with perceptions of our civilization over the last 150 years and in days to come. There are frequent attempts to express feelings in abstract form. There are one or two old masters and other works set against them in contrast. And there are vast works of imagination.

A lot of it is knockdown art. It is iconoclastic, intended to shock, knock us off our perches, destroy previously conceived images, invade the ivory towers of comfort and soothing we all build around ourselves. It's aim is to disturb, turn us around to look at ourselves, at beauty and form, in fresh ways. It's subversive. There are also things that blow your mind and make you wonder at the sheer scale of creative imagination - how could someone ever conceive that...........so different, so amazing.

If we want someone to pat us on the tummy, put an arm round our complacency and say 'there, there', Tate Modern is definitely not the place to go even if it is free. There is not a lot of nostalgia here for the old days (were they ever that good?) but there is much about what we as human beings (a)have become and (b) might yet be and reach out for.

Many of the artists on display feel impelled to do what they do. They can't help themselves. It's a drive, an intensity, the way they see life and want others to see and know. A true calling they cannot resist. A sort of priesthood. Ordained to do what they have to do. Just as a Spanish T.V. cameraman murdered a few years ago in an ambush in Sierra Leone, believed he had been ordained to live on the front line of the world's dangerous and evil places and report back. It is the same, just as some feel called to be priests of Church, or rabbis, or to worship in temple or mosque. It is a must, to deny it would be to deny their true selves.

But Tate Modern is a godly Cathedral all right. Be sure that it is an act of God's creation as sure as the first chapter of the bible. Going inside I found myself overwhelmed by the sheer weight of humanity. It is an act of faith in humanity rather than the God we have been weaned on through the centuries and brought up on until now. It is a Temple of the Spirit though we may bring too much 'Christian' or other baggage with us to recognise it.

The true Holy Spirit disturbs more than it comforts. It is iconoclastic, breaking down the idols we have made, requiring us to look at ourselves again. It is subversive which is why God-believers are nearly always the first target of attack by governments or regimes unsure of themselves. It is a truly modern Cathedral because God is not mentioned, for this is where we are now. We are in an age looking for faith yet disbelieving so many of the images of God that have been presented to us. Rightly so. We are discovering, slowly, painfully, that the real God is one who is present in the heart of human life yet remains hidden. One of the ancient saints said that Life with God was a game of hide and seek. Sometimes God coughs or chuckles to let you know that he(?) is there, uniquely personal to each of us, yet remains hidden.

In the 21st Century you really have to look for this God. The ages of pictures of God being handed to us on a plate are over and the beginning and the end of it is this, that the only way we can find God is in the hidden depths of the human heart. Usually it's the last place where we think of looking.

P.S. And I tell you what - at this Cathedral the whole world was there - high and low, rich and poor, all colours, all creeds, rough and ready, smart and suave, ancient and modern -just crowds.

<u>Everybody's got one</u>

Eternal Life (life after death?) How do you fancy a bit, a slice of eternal life right now? Right! O.K! miracles I can do straightaway, explanations take a bit longer.

I'm not talking about living for ever (immortality) that would be hell. Eternal Life you have now whether you recognise it or not. You don't have to be religious either to have it or spot it. You don't have to wait for it. It's like your finger prints, printed in, unique to you, except that it's also there when you're dead and gone.

Everybody has it, everybody's got one, an eternal life. It's not quite what the nurse meant when she said to the male patient standing by his bed (opposite mine) without his pyjama legs, 'Don't bother Albert, when you've seen one you've seen them all', but you get the drift. Everyone has it. She told him to cover himself up and sadly that's what we do with eternal life. We do it with the wrong ideas we've absorbed into our skin from the world we live in.

So how do you spot it, this eternal life? By stopping being attached to things, clinging to things. Anything. Everything - possessions, people, ego dreams and pictures, ideas and beliefs; holding on to anything that lulls us into a false sense of security. We have to learn to be unstuck. We are Clingons. And this also stops us from being happy.

We cling on to ideas about money, reputation - oh! how we like to be thought well of- we cling to the notion that to be acceptable to others we have to dress in a certain way, have certain possessions; and we soon get uppity if someone doesn't conform, does not do or say the things that are acceptable to us.

Of course we have friends and loved ones whom it is right to stand up for, but to cling on to them is living death for them and for us: the children whose lives as adults have been ruined because of the fixed expectations parents had of them. Marriages which have been ruined because of the pedestal one partner placed another on, clinging to fantasy year after year; and marriages which have been saved because both partners learned to change and be transformed by the flesh and blood presence of the other.

We live so frequently in 'if only land'. 'If onlys' are packed with the semtex of unhappiness. They bring grudge, grunge, disappointments galore. They explode in our faces disfiguring us and blinding us to eternal life. A woman clings onto her grief for a husband ten years dead (if only he were still alive). One of the most loving things we can ever say to another human being who is precious to us is, 'Don't cling to me'.

There was a man who was becoming blind. Nothing could stop it. It was a terrible struggle (if only I wasn't going blind). His picture of himself and his relationships with others, his future, all ruined. His features were twisted with bitterness and anger. He didn't want to give up what he had had and learn life all over again. They had said to him, try to accept it, learn to welcome what is inevitable. Slowly, slowly, he learnt to go with the flow until one day it was as if he decided to put his arm round his blindness and say, 'Welcome friend'. He smiled, his sight had gone of course but his face was transformed, became quite lovely. This is eternal life

We cling to flesh and bone. Eternal life is a power, a presence in the soul that touches neither. Everybody's got one, whatever the gender! How often we hear this noble human story told by someone who had to let go of everything - 'I'd come to the end of my tether. And I just don't know where I got the strength from but I did'. Or 'I felt a presence, a power'.

Happiness is about being ready to let go and move on. To stop clinging. Happiness is always on the hoof, here and now, not then and there. Today, this moment. Or not at all. And eternal life is found in the same place. So we may even have to revise our anxieties, terrors, hopes about what death actually is. Dust to dust for certain, yet with that final letting go what 'happiness' may then await?

Be sure, though, that it will not fit any present definition.

Silence and Stillness - We are what we do with Silence

I'm at it again. I can't leave it alone really. Well, it's Silence. You've noticed of course. I mean, if its getting to you, you don't have to read on; whenever I got my harp out at home and started harping on, one of my daughters would quietly start singing - 'boring, boring'.

Silence. That's it. Weird, having to use words to usher in Silence, but that's because there's not enough of it around and we need a bit of a word-map to find the lost treasure. I wonder, perhaps, if schools should teach Silence. You might say it's the missing dimension in education. Switch off the computer, come off the website, stop texting, dowse the telly, kill the DVD. Ban the car radio. Put the book down. Stop trying to explain. For a while - two minutes wouldn't be a bad start. Imagine a whole school coming to silence for two minutes a week. Not much? It would have its effect.

Silence, why? Because words without silence are meaningless. Without silence we become a babbling, incoherent mob. The world learns more in the two-minutes silence at Remembrance (in November) than from a whole bookshop of sermons.

There was a lovely moment the other evening in Maryport (if you haven't been to Maryport to watch sunsets you haven't lived). I noticed in the far distance, a young man sitting silently on his own just looking out across the Solway as the sun reluctantly made its way down behind the Scottish hills. As I quietly drew level, he just looked up for a moment and smiled and said "Good, eh?" Some two-minutes silence.

In the beginning, Silence, Stillness and Silence. We have grown out of the mystery whose name is Silence. Everything that has ever become history since that aeon time was held in that silence. Words grew out of the silence, not to banish but to enhance it. We all start in silence, we all come out of a space, our own inner space, the womb-space. With all that we know, it is still mysterious and dark in there.

Silence is respect. Respect for each other's space. More than that, it is self-respect, respect of our own inner space. We cannot enter it without silence. It is the core, the whole switch-on of our being. We need to be in touch with the mystery of our beginnings: there is so much there waiting to be discovered. Silence is the world waiting to be born out of the mystery of our human past. 'We cannot go on happily for long if we are out of touch with the hidden springs of our spiritual life'. (Thomas Merton)

The Holy Ones have always, always, said the same: 'the thought of God is the silence of the mind'. 'There is nothing so much like God as silence'. A present-day holy man:- 'The most important and obvious thing about God is that he is silent. He does not speak. He does not grunt, or shuffle his feet, or cough, or do anything to assure us that he is there. He meets us in his silence - what the Church needs is people who believe in shutting up; that God is not a talking God; that we do not have the word of God, we have the silence of God'. And he concludes, "So I'll shut up". (JohnFenton)

The grandchild has just started school. She and her youngish grandma were on holiday in our fells. High up they came upon a small pond with one perfect water-lily floating in it. "Can we sit down?" asks the child. So they sit at the edge of the water for a short rest. Forty five minutes on and they are still sitting, gazing without any comment or interruption. Then slowly the child says things about being at school and what it's like. In a bit, Grandma says, "Shall we go now?" "Let's look at the water-lily just a little longer," says the child. On returning the child rushes over to father, "Oh, daddy, we've had such a lovely time. We've been watching a water-lily". Grandma pictured the scene that might have happened had father been with them, with his keen mind. She pictured him saying, "Yes, it's a water-lily, and its Latin name is Nymphaea and it's very rare in these parts. Let's go higher up and see how many more we can find and then tell the Warden all about it". A few weeks later grandchild writes to Grandma "We did have a lovely holiday didn't we Granny? I think of the water-lily every night before I go to sleep".(Wanda Nash)

Mostly, children have an innocence which they take with them, wide-eyed and fresh, to school, rising up out of their still untarnished inner space. Those little ones, going, say, for their first time - O! brave new world. Education's task is to keep that innocence bright, but it can so easily sink it.

Silence and innocence go together. Silence can restore innocence and freshness day by day to jaded adults, penetrating the broken promises and shattered dreams. No, I didn't say it was easy, but innocence restored? Oh, yes, I do say it's possible and worth it. We are what we do with Silence.

THE SEASONS

Christmas 1 - Anyone would think you lived in a cave!

"Kevin! O my God Kevin! Have you seen your room, it's disgusting! Anyone would think you lived in a cave. What a hole!" Irate mother on entering son's room. Could just as easily be Tracey, mind.

One of the funniest Christmas cards I ever received was years ago when what was called The Women's Movement was in full flower. The picture was a cave with a big star above and, outside, camels, wise men, shepherds, a donkey - all the usual things. A woman emerges from the cave and announces triumphantly, "It's a girl".

A cave. The point here is that it was a cave. Scholars will tell us that maybe Jesus was born not in a cunningly illuminated-by-the-Star shining-through-the-rafters-stable but in a cave. In the back of the cave - the animals would be kept at the front. That's how it was for the poorest of the poor around Bethlehem and other places those days. A cave, simple, bare, dark. Perhaps this fits the truth about Jesus better today. It takes off the tinsel, the cosy glitz. It takes the straw off the floor. Luke, the only one in the bible who tells the story about the stable and the manger and the swaddling clothes (I love that phrase) is trying to get home the idea that Jesus was born in the roughest, lowest place, down-town, on the other side of the tracks. Where you would never think of going or looking. And that is good news.

The monks were praying that their saintly leader who was dying, would go and be with Jesus in heaven. "Oh no!" he said, "pray for me to go to hell. I shall be sure to find Jesus there".

But there is another cave. Holy men and women all down the ages, in all the religions of the world, have talked about the cave of the human heart. Go, they say, rest quietly there, and you will discover all you need to know. Deep, deep in the core of every human being is this dark mysterious unknown place. Here, somehow, the hopes and fears of all the years are met together, all centuries from the beginning of time shunt up against each other. This is the mystery of every human being born.

I AM not 'just out of mummy's tummy'. I AM not just a combination of genes. I AM is more sacred than that. God-searching people

104

believe that the spirit of the universe dwells in every human heart and in silence is loving to all.

The spirit of Jesus, of God, is born in the cave of every human heart even before Jesus was born. The Spirit of the Universe is within us. You are the holy crib. The Star shines in you. The Christmas card is just an outside picture of how it really is within.

Travel in and discover your true self enshrouded in the afterbirth of the spirit of the universe which Jesus models for us. Coming out on the catwalk of history, he's modelling living and dying, and loving, all that miracle. The show begins December 25th, but it doesn't end there.

Travel in. Don't be afraid of your darkness, even if it feels inferior, down the other side of the tracks. If you are looking for the best Christmas present for yourself or anyone who has everything. When they gathered, these visitors, that first Christmas, they each in their own way said, 'Isn't he divine!' If you are patient enough to stay awhile in the cave of your heart, you will hear the same words. That's the gift you have been given. No exceptions. Kevin, isn't he divine! Tracey, isn't she divine!

Happy Christmas present.

INTERLUDE

'He was born in a borrowed stable,
taught from a borrowed book,
fed five thousand people with a borrowed loaf,
rode into Jerusalem on a borrowed donkey,
celebrated the last supper in a borrowed room,
borrowed the strength of a stranger
to carry his cross
and was finally buried in a borrowed tomb'.

(Edward Patey - one time Dean of Liverpool Anglican Cathedral)

Hooray for Harry Potter

Hooray for Harry Potter! What a way to begin a new year! - or any day of the year ! But why? Because the way in which, in every book, the very ordinary words and phrases of everyday language are used and reach places in the human heart that more hackneyed and often pompous words at present do not reach. So Harry Potter is read by millions across the world, in perhaps 30 different languages. Harry Potter expresses where people are in the struggle between good and evil and which is revealed as deeper and more full of mystery than just at surface level: the books echo our fears as many of us peer out into the new year, hardly daring it to begin; the risks to human life and civilisation seem so many and escalating. People all over are exploring the mystery with fear and horror yet also with awe and wonder. This is what the magic of Harry Potter is about, the unexpectedness both of good and evil.

What many believe is happening is that we are moving (being transformed?) into a higher plane of conscious awareness where everything is more starkly revealed; particularly the good and bad which bind us all together. Down the ages spiritual writers and strugglers, with an enlightened view of humankind, of all faiths and none, have made it clear, that seeing more sharply the good way to choose, the more intense and intimate the presence of evil also appears, in us and around us.

Another picture. We trudge up fells, climb mountains reaching out with a sense of satisfaction to the beauty and wonder we pass on the way, and see sometimes in greater splendour everywhere around, at the summit on a clear day. Bur also the sharper, the harder the climb, the more dangerous it can be. Black heavens can so easily envelop us, swiftly looming out of nowhere -mists, slipperiness, shapes, scrambles, obstacles not bargained for, sudden threatening challenges. It takes courage often to continue upwards. What started out as good can become menacing, even life-threatening. This metaphor is not perfect but you get the meaning. There is only one way to go if you have to get there; facing it, trusting your inner self.

Harry Potter shows the way (remember the magic, the wizards and the wands, the spells, potions and lotions, are really a sideline, on the surface; another metaphor of things that may beguile and beset us, dazzle and tempt us, try a bit of this, a bit of that). All the books are a parable. What Harry Potter does is what we must latch onto as we walk day by day, facing what's there, with so much that is uncertain and unknown. What does Harry Potter do? Well, he fights for his life but never takes revenge or knowingly the life of another. He seems always to offer forgiveness, never sets out to destroy. 'Love' is the very word; Voldemort (The Black Wizard, the Epitome of Evil) sneers at it unrelentingly. And in our deepest hearts, though we may neglect it, we know that 'love' is true, the only way to go. In Harry Potter, Dumbledore (The Wizard of Universal Kindness) says "You are the true master of death, because the true master does not seek to run away from Death. He accepts that he must die, and understands that there are far, far worse things in the living world than dying............ Do not pity the dead, Harry. Pity the living, and, above all, those who live without love".

Hooray for Harry Potter. Invented but real. Made in the likeness of God.

<u>Getting away from it all</u>

No sooner has New Year drawn its first breath, yawned and stretched, when the bombardment to get away from it all begins. Ho, ho, holidays! Sunkissed summer brochures, gorgeous discounts if you want to get tanned in the right places. 'If you got the money, honey and you got the time..........' the world is your oyster. The lure of distant places, the magic, the enticement to journeys away, journeys into the unknown. Whether Benidorm, Canadian Capers, Seychelles, Fiji, Unkleshparkanbrechen (ah! you don't know where that is do you?) Those precious holidays.

But don't be fooled my lovelies. The Wise Ones have things to say about journeys and holidays. They will tell you that holiday means Holy Day and that every day is to be made a holiday. The search is certainly on, we want to know more, see more, experience more. Yet the Wise One said to the world-traveller, "Stay in your cell and I will teach you all you ever need to know". The traveller replied "I'm no monk and anyway I don't have a cell". "Of course you have a cell", was the reply, "and you can enter there any time you wish. Look within".

Madame Vanity Fair refused to acknowledge the passing of the years. She was applying more suntan lotion on a far distant shore and someone asked her what her age was. "I really don't know", she said, "it keeps changing every minute". She had not travelled very far. True freedom is not away from it all, running around topless or facing a rugged challenging encounter up some alp or down some hole, though that may help from time to time.

True freedom is making every day a sacred holy day by the way we are and live moment by moment.

Dag Hammarskjold, as Secretary General of United Nations in the 50s' journeyed constantly across the surfaces of the world, always high-profile, always in the public eye at momentous meetings in the world's big places. In his diary he wrote, 'The longest journey is the journey inward..........the more faithfully you listen to the voice within you, the better you will hear what is sounding outside'.

So an ancient Jewish tale. Isaac lived in Cracow, Poland. He kept having a dream which told him to journey to faraway Prague and dig under the bridge that led to the royal palace, where he would find hidden treasure. To begin with he thought nothing of it, but the dream recurred so frequently that he eventually decided to take it seriously.

He came at last at the bridge to discover, to his dismay, that it was closely guarded. He didn't know what to do, but kept presenting himself at the bridge each morning. The captain of the guard became suspicious and asked him his business. Embarrassed Isaac told him about the dream. The captain roared with laughter and said, "Heavens, where would we all be if we all took our dreams so seriously. I keep having one - why I don't know - but I would be stupid to do anything about it. In my dream I hear a voice which tells me to go all the way to Cracow, find a Jew called Isaac, and dig up the corner of his kitchen. If I did I would find buried treasure. Fancy that, how stupid!" And he went away laughing his head off.

Stunned, Isaac turned round and made his way home. There he dug up the corner of his kitchen and found a treasure abundant enough to keep him in comfort until the day he died.

Have a lovely time this year, going hither and thither, doing this and that. Only don't forget to read the signpost which points to You-in-Your-Own-Backyard. You are sacred, you are holy ground, you yourself are treasure beyond price. The most important journey we all make is the one we make every day.

Lent - Old and New

She looked fantastic when we met again. "Hey! you look just great!" I said, not quite able to spot exactly the difference. "Weightwatchers" she replied "I lost X hundredweights (joke) in Y weeks". She had then been fasting, depriving herself of certain foods, indeed of a certain way of life, in order to trim herself up.

A member of our family goes on a detox diet from time to time to 'purify' her system and feel better, livelier, stronger. People adopt a training discipline to compete, hopefully perhaps to win a prize, or jog for charity. Doing without in order to gain something better. Note the word 'discipline' in this context. It means to learn, to be taught or to teach yourself something about yourself.

If you are not 'in' the Church you would not really know this but the Church is now in a fasting season called Lent (from Ash Wednesday to Easter Day). It is supposed to mirror the 40 days described both in the Old Testament (Moses up a mountain without food, etc.) and in the New Testament when Jesus went to live in the harsh deprivations of a wilderness for 40 days to learn more deeply how to discipline himself to live the ways of God in daily life. Only 40 years ago, this fasting time in the churches I attended was quite severe.

There would be no flowers at all anywhere during Lent and the altar and any crucifixes might be covered with sackcloth or purple drapes as a sign of sorrow for sins committed and a determination to be more disciplined, to 'do better' in the Christian way. And sorry, folks, no weddings at all during Lent. I well remember the anger, the frustration and sheer sad disappointment of couples who had set their hearts on a spring wedding (reclaiming a year's tax before April came in was one of the reasons). One church I belonged to had softened this a bit, allowing weddings and flowers, but the flowers had to be brought in and out on the wedding day; nothing was to disturb the grim fact of piety through these 40 days. Retirement homes benefitted. It also used to be no meat, just fish, on a Friday, often missing one meal completely one day a week, or one meal every day of the week. Going to church for some extra devotions and courses.

Many churchgoers don't now pay much attention to the idea of fasting. We may decide no chocolates, no alcohol (yes, no sex for some) and to put 5p pieces in a special bottle in the kitchen. There is also more likely to be a Lent lunch in an ecumenical church hall (a bowl of soup and a piece of bread for which you donate a £1, or whatever, as solidarity, with the world's poor). If you are lucky two bowls of soup if there is any left over and butter substitute on the bread, and a biscuit perhaps. And maybe afterwards, if you are still hungry, you may go home and have a proper lunch (been there, done that!).

It is meant to be a 'purifying', a cleansing of the body, mind and spirit, yet if this fasting is only an outward sign, a nod to keep on the right side of God, with no change of heart or earnestness to move inwardly towards a deeper place of faith, it is of course meaningless. A bit like slowing down for the speed camera and then zooming up and off again afterwards. Almost irresponsible you might say – "aren't I good!" - a whole six weeks without chocolate and now I can tuck in again, munch, munch.

Anyway to be a disciple, a learner, is not an easy business, however you go about it. And most like to read this memo about the disciples Jesus chose. It may cheer you up a bit. If you belong. If you don't, perhaps you will be a bit more gentle with those who do.

MEMORANDUM

To: Jesus, Son of Joseph
From: Jordan Management Consultants, Jerusalem

Dear Sir

Thank you for submitting the names of the twelve men you have picked for management in your new organisation. All of them have now taken our battery of tests; we have not only run the results through our computer but also arranged personal interviews for each of them with our psychologist and vocational aptitude consultant.

111

It is the staff opinion that most of your nominees are lacking in background, education and vocational aptitude for the type of enterprises you are undertaking. They do not have the team concept. We would recommend that you continue your search for persons of experience in managerial ability and proven capabilities.

Simon Peter is emotionally unstable and given to fits of temper. Andrew has absolutely no qualities of leadership. The two brothers, James and John, the sons of Zebedee, place personal interest above company loyalty. Thomas demonstrates a questioning attitude that would tend to undermine morale. We feel that it is our duty to tell you that Matthew has been blacklisted by the Greater Jerusalem Better Business Bureau. James, the son of Alphaeus, and Thaddeus definitely have radical leanings, and they both registered a high score on the manic-depressive scale.

One of the candidates, however, shows great potential He is a man of ability and resourcefulness, meets people well, has a keen business mind and has contacts in high places. He is highly motivated, ambitious and responsible. We recommend Judas Iscariot as your controller and right-hand man. All of the other profiles are self-explanatory.

We wish you every success in your new venture.

Yours sincerely

Jordan Management Consultants.

The Weight of Glory

You are 'filth'. This is how some extremist Muslims regard
Christians, Jews, indeed all our culture and the rest of the world;
except Muslims. It sounds bad, it is bad. Hang on though. It is
equally bad to call, in more polite phrases, the world 'damned' or
'lost' as some extremist Christians do. What do you call 'filth' and
why?

However this needs to be read:-
The savagery of the attacks on Christians in Iraq is becoming
almost unspeakable.
Three examples from the month of October 2006:
(1) A 14 year old boy in Basra was crucified.
(2) A church minister was kidnapped in Mosul and while his
family were trying to raise the ransom, his body was discovered,
with head, hands and feet cut off and arranged carefully on his
torso
(3) A 3 year old child was kidnapped in Baghdad and, because her
mother was too poor to pay a ransom, the child was returned to
her, beheaded, roasted and served on a bed of rice.

This is utter depravity. It is the heart of darkness. I want to run a
million miles, but it's no good. This is our generation, our times,
and we have to live it. First, if you are a person who prays (and
we do not run away though we may want to) it's where prayer
takes us, deep, deep down to face the fears and evils of the world
which are always threatening to overwhelm us. All peoples have
perpetually to struggle towards the light anyway. So often I feel
that the Church, and I am part of it, skiddles around on the surface
of things. Lots of people outside the Church think the same but
this is where those who regard themselves as committed to
Christian faith have to go, again and again, the heart of darkness.

113

Now, in April, the Church is limbering up for Good Friday and Easter. The symbol is Jesus, a man, 'filth' to those who crucified him (and they were believers). I believe no sensitive person inside or outside the Church can escape that person because that persona is also in ourselves, part of the DNA of being human. It is that part of the human calling, the sacred core that can lead anyone to the light in life. We do have the inner resources as human beings to find the courage to be there, and confront. But not with violence for violence. Love, the innocent Jesus shows, crucified for love of the world, is the weight of glory. The weight.

Creation, living in the world, is meant to be full of glory. And it is, it is, beyond our 'filth'. But weight needs lifting up and all are called to do this, for love of the world. Good Friday was real. Every Friday is real. Easter Sunday was real. Every Sunday is real for it reveals that at the heart of this life is the glory of an eternal life. Love discovered, whenever, however, wherever, is the start of eternal life here and now, and it will be discovered again and again by all who seek to lift and carry the weight of glory.

My Flesh and Blood

Blood. It's all about blood. Blood spilt for the sake of others. Bloody Good Friday. For Christians the day Jesus died. History is littered with heroic figures of faith and no one figure has dominated this country more than Jesus, indeed the whole of Europe and western civilisation. Everywhere you find crosses and crucifixes. People wear them as jewellery or good luck charms. We will visit sacred sites, we will gawp at cathedrals. Some places of Christian heritage strike us dumb with awe, there is such a sense of presence there. All because - a fact of history -one man died.

I was watching the film 'Gandhi' again recently and at one point the clergyman who is following Gandhi is helped to clamber onto the roof of a train by Hindu fellow-travellers. They see his dog-collar and one of them says, "Oh, you drink blood don't you?" He looked a bit perplexed until the man said, "You know, the body and blood of Christ".

I have heard Christians accused of cannibalism. I have seen people turn away in disgust because of this 'drinking blood' thing - which of course for aeons of time many actually did at ancient religious ceremonies (and here and there still do) believing it pleased the gods and/or gave them the god's strength to do battle with life. Washing in the blood of the first-born (sometimes the great sacrifice was to give a child, a symbol of untarnished innocence, usually it was a first-born calf or goat or lamb, etc.) was thought to be a way of cleansing. 'Washed in the blood of the Lamb' is still a phrase some Christians use.

The Blood, the Body and Blood of Christ, the Mass, the Communion, the Eucharist, whatever name you give it is the heart of Christian faith - weird to the onlooker, central to the believer. It is something actual and physical Christians do in worship. Bread and wine (body and blood) are made sacred in worship and believers take them into themselves because they desire most earnestly to clear out of the way the things that seem to separate them from God; to belong to God and be more godlike in life, or more simply to be more like Jesus. It is not paying your dues, it's not earning merit, getting on the good side, it's not nudging you along the golden road, it is an act of devotion.

It can look casual. Of course it can be casual. It can mean next to nothing, a holy cafeteria, everyone lining up, a take it or leave it sort of thing. It can be entered into out of fear; if you don't do this God the Bully will get you. It can be and usually is, an act of deep devotion, taking into yourself the Life of another Being and by that act being transformed. An outward sign of something happening inside; an inward grace, a gift given. A faith that everyone has in them the potential to become divine, not God but as God.

It is a sacred thing, a sacrament. The receiving of the Body and Blood is not for everybody but it is not to be despised. And because ordinary things, bread and wine, (the staff of life) are transmuted in the worship, it's meant to be a dead ordinary thing to do. It is meant to say to us that everything ordinary can be seen to be filled with God's presence; everything ordinary is also sacred, can become a sacrament. Yes the humble butty, yes the washing-up, yes cutting the hedge and cleaning the car, yes sweeping the street. Life is sacred, the Body and the Blood are saying that everything, if you look through it, can bring you closer to God. God is in the ordinary, every present moment; every here-and-now moment is a sacrament.

Syd was 95, this West Cumbrian, when I knew him. He had been a rough diamond in his time, sharp, sometimes hard I suspect. Anyway not always an easy man. In his last days he once said to me - he came to church regularly – "the only thing that matters is the bread and the wine". I went to give him communion once in hospital. He was in a two-bedded ward and there was a man in the other bed with visitors. It was clear they didn't really know what we were about. My friend was a small, slight man, now quite frail. So we began whilst the others sort of looked on. We said a few words together then he began to weep. He went on to weep most of the time we were doing the communion thing, we had to keep stopping and waiting. I could see the other group looking on in mystified horror - how could a priest of the Church do this to such a frail old man in hospital causing him to suffer so?

And so it went on for some time. They had stopped talking and were just staring at us. Then finally he took the bread and the wine made sacred, the Body and Blood, and looking up with a tear-stained face he said, "Isn't it glorious!"

A sacrament takes you deeper into the mystery of being alive at all. In the end, all is mystery. Don't be afraid of The Mystery. It doesn't all end in tears, or blood. It does end in glory, and not just for the faithful few. Easter is not just about Easter bunnies.

INTERLUDE

A Christian Devotion

I see his blood upon the rose,
And in the stars the glory of his eyes,
His body gleams amid eternal snows,
His tears fall from the skies.

I see his face in every flower;
The thunder and the singing of the birds
Are but his voice - and carven by his power
Rocks are written words.

All pathways by his feet are worn,
His strong heart stirs the ever-beating sea,
His crown of thorns is twined with every thorn,
His cross is every tree.

(Joseph Plunkett -1887 to 1916)

Equality with God

I feel rather like a doorkeeper or bouncer at the House of God for this is an Easter exclusive. To those who aren't in the club and don't want to believe in God, I say, come along for the ride by all means, you may be interested. But what's going on here today is a bit of 'in-talk' for those who say they believe in the Christian picture of God. I want to ask the so-called Jesus-people what do they think they believe when they go on about Resurrection, Easter and all the rest.

I don't know whether you are ready for this or whether I am just being arrogant (superior!) and telling my grandmother how to suck eggs. Is this something you have really known in your heart of hearts all along? I would love to know - speak to me, Horatio or Henrietta or whoever you are. In this little procession of words that follows, I would really like to know if you think I've gone off my Christian rocker.

Jesus died, right? 'To save us from our sins?' Well, O.K. And 'now sits enthroned in heaven on the right hand of God?' Well, yes, I suppose so, but all in all it's a pretty dull and negative way of talking about Easter - and for me, not too highly important in the list of explanations.

I would rather say - proclaim, shout out loud if you like - that Jesus died to show us that we are in Heaven already. The stars are already in our eyes. All the way to heaven is heaven. We are born with it in us.

Deep, deep inside ourselves, within the silence of silences, beyond all alleluias and Lord have mercys and woe-is-mes; beyond any names or shapes or descriptions, there is in us a place where time never penetrates, a huge still space or darkness. It is darkness because it is far too deep for any description to reach or know.

It is here, in this part of ourselves, that we have common ground with God. Here is our secret, buried in us before we were born, that we are given equality with God. 'Come, be with me, where I am' is the Word, dwelling within. Here we can find our own divinity. This place is so sacred that even God takes his shoes off. No separation here. The equality that was given us at the start, as birthright gift. The gift above all gifts. If you have life, whoever, whatever you are, all creatures great and small, you have this gift. It is the meaning of everything. God is always far nearer to us than we ever dare to think.

This is eternal life. This is what Jesus died for - to show that Heaven, the one thing we all seem to want, is already ours. You don't have to earn it, fight your way to get there, get a map from the A.A., score brownie points. Nothing like that at all. You don't have to wait to die before you experience it. And not even the worst sufferings can separate us from it.

We are far too occupied with sin and guilt. Concentrating on them is a bit like going in for a GCSE expecting no more than a 'D' after all your hard work, when you have already been given a brilliant 'A' with no work at all. Sin and some guilt are important but not all that important.

There are some loving, wise and holy people around who show me this all the time. They gently describe themselves as stained or tarnished. They may have made serious mistakes but they don't seem to care very much. What they certainly have, no matter how old they are, is abundant youthfulness. They say – "One of the difficulties about being old is that I feel so young". All they are saying is that the eternal presence of God, which has been there since the beginning, is bubbling up in them. It's irrepressible. To live with such internal sprightliness is to live in eternal life and taste equality with God.

No Richter scale to measure this of course but listen to these young old people and how they see things. They see that everything somehow belongs together - has a unity. They are not put off, though sorrowful, by the terrors and traps of the world, and are able to see more and more the presence of God in and through everything. Yes, even in crucifixion.

Even when Jesus on the cross is given the words 'My God, my God why have you forsaken me?' God is clearly nearer than he is able to think or know - or there would have been no Resurrection.

That's what Easter's about. Enjoy life, everything every moment, but live as if you are already dead. In that way you won't hang on to things you have to let go of anyway, eventually. Don't worry too much about being dead. Yes we lose all things that we see, hear, smell, touch, taste but this is only the beginning of beginnings. The golden thread that has held you in eternal presence all your flesh and bone life long, does not snap when you die.

It is more blessed to receive this gift than to give any other gift to anybody else in our lifetime. It is only when we can completely accept this gift that we can then give our life to others. For love. As Jesus did.

To my many dear friends who do not believe in Christ or God and yet live lives of love and hope, this (from one of the ancient poems of the bible, Psalm 17): 'When you wake up in your own new dawn, you will find the energy, the power, the love of the universe (call it what you will) standing next to you in a way you will recognise. And you will be satisfied'.

INTERLUDE

I want you to be happy, always happy in the
Lord; I repeat, what I want is your happiness.
Let your tolerance be evident to everyone: the
Lord is very near. There is no need to worry;
but if there is anything you need, pray for it,
asking God for it with prayer and thanksgiving,
and that peace of God, which is so much greater
than we can understand, will guard your hearts and your
thoughts, in Christ Jesus.

(Philippians Ch.4 vv.4,5,6 & 7)

I'm all of an alleluia

A time for Wonder - O Microsoft, Supersoft, Internet, and Galactic conversations. Fax me a love letter. 'When our Kevin phones from Australia I can hear him clearer than when you phone from Cleator'.

A time for wonder, a time for amazement, but not of these things. They are playthings, gewgaws, clever though they are. They are like the first clumsy movements of a person who has broken the hand they normally write with and is having to use the other.

What is a wonder, for example, is the coming in of autumn and how, in the next few days, we shall continually be breath-taken and dazzled by the changing array of colours we capture through our eyes.

The eye. I remember the first time my first child tottered on his two legs 10 feet across the room to me. Over 100 million sense cells in each eye ensured that he walked towards the safety of my arms.

There are cells in the eye which are cones and cells which are rods- 7 million cones and just over 100 million rods. The rods report what they see only in black and white; the cones fire off messages to the brain which give awareness of colour. Because of the cones we can distinguish between at least 1,000 shades of colour. Welcome to autumn.

Even so, we miss most of what there is to see. The eye has to be selective if the brain is not to be confused. So two people painting the same scene will paint it differently. Look at the variety of paintings of Ennerdale or Maryport Harbour which adorn many homes in my part of the world. We focus on what we choose to notice and so gradually build up our own picture of the world and make it our own. No one else sees it quite the same way.

Then there's all that coordination that goes on between hand and eye to paint the picture or put this pen continually to paper. When I simply flex my hand open and shut I use 70 different muscles. 'The narrowest hinge on my hand puts to scorn all machinery'. (Walt Whitman)

In all the colours of this dying time we perhaps remember the first days of spring, plants planted, seeds sown. Certainly this year people will remember the long, unending it seemed, blue, hot summer days. And in ten years' time too.

Autumn and Harvest. Autumn is a time for harvesting memories. Older people are in the autumn of their life. There is a recalling of all the faces and places known and visited. All to be found in the place called memory, a substance soft as toothpaste stashed away in the head with little threads of nerve fibre running down between the nerve cells. Here in an instant we can project on our tiny internal screen all the pictures of a lifetime. Old granny has stored away in there a video recorder no money can ever buy.

This is wonder, this is amazement - the mystery of how I am made, held together in all the myriad parts that go to make up the action man called me. Wonder at being alive, alive at all, surviving all this time right up to now.

I say "I AM" and a million electrical impulses flash and dance around my body without my ever thinking about it.

Autumn is to be in awe of the gift of life which is me. It is the counting of blessings, collecting and harvesting them! It is not a time for bemoaning what I have not done, or what no longer works.

I AM. I have had life. And in addition there has been bread in my belly, a bed to rest on, a roof to shelter me, the light of each new day, and some who have loved me more than I will ever know - for all or part of the time. And I am only one.

This is not a lament. It's me, bewildered, all-of-an-alleluia-inside. And if this was not enough, the end which harvest and autumn proclaim is pointing us forward. There are signals, messages for us in every cell, every fibre, every atom of our bodies and all of creation if we want to hear. A deafening chorus of encouragement beaming in.

Rabindranach Tagore, a 20th century Indian poet:- 'I have kissed this

122

world with my eyes and my limbs; I have wrapt it within my heart in numerous folds; I have flooded its days and nights with thoughts till the world and my life have grown one - and I love my life because I love the light of the sky so en woven with me'.

As we are all slowly dying, hopefully with a repeated giving of thanks, the cycle of seasons is secretly singing its song of the universe. Listen to it saying - 'Life will come again'. Read it with hope from the natural world if you cannot stomach the personal messages of religion.

All this gradual fading of colours is a rebirthing. Spring, your spring, will come again. Not only will the grass grow once more but the marvel that goes into the making of one human eye, one human memory, that marvel will be magnified a million, billion, trillion times into the explosion of life which waits beyond this death. Marvel upon marvel. Only do not be afraid. All shall be well.

This is the great and mighty Wonder.

INTERLUDE

Know that from the darkness of the earth life there springs and flourishes that which flowers in beauty, giving forth perfume and radiance. And so we say that whatever may be our circumstances or your troubles at this present time, be thankful; for they are the soil about your roots from which the blossoms will spring forth in due season.

(Wisdom from White Eagle)

Get rid of God

"I pray to God to rid me of God" - the words of a holy Christian man called Meister Eckhart who caused a great stir way back in the 13th/14th centuries. A holy riddle. But we need to hear these words again and again and learn to believe them.

So much harm has been done by religions trying to fix God. Whenever we try to give the name 'God' to God then that is not God. God is a naked God who has no name. A holy riddle.

All scriptures of all religions tell us <u>about</u> God, and that is all. The Hindus remind us that 'all scripture means as much as a water-tank in a universal flood'. They are just the signposts to the motorway but oh! so often are confused with the motorway itself. 'God' says the Hindu, 'is what the dark is when the last lamp is blown out'.

I'm not trying to make it harder to believe but easier. If you believe in a God you can see or touch or feel or think - what sort of God is that in the end? Just an idol or an icon like a golden cross, or a statue of the Virgin or a bottle of holy water, a piece of wood or a stone. Precious (to you), beautiful, important perhaps to you, but only a signpost. Each is only one very small view of God.

I think of the numbers of people who, when they lived in one place, loved the church there, every stone of it, and went for years and years until they moved to a new place, a new town. Then they stopped. It's as if they equated God with one particular building which felt special. Or with a particular job they did in the name of St. Saviour's, Humpty Dumpty Town. When the job stopped they stopped. They may know about God; what do they know of God?

It's like saying my home is a terraced or a semi-detached des..res. This is not a home, it's a description. What makes it a home is hidden, a mystery - it certainly isn't bloomers on the line or videos in the bookcase. A small house I used to visit was a tip, it could hardly be anything else with a mum and dad and 9 children, but you knew it was a home as soon as you walked through the door.

Meister Eckhart says God is like someone with whom you are playing hide and seek, who coughs to let you know he's there but remains hidden. He also says talking about God and putting this before silence with God is a sin. (beware all clergy, rabbis, mullahs and preachy persons - which includes me).

Let me say the Holy Riddle again. In order to know God we have to keep on emptying ourselves of all we know about God. We have to believe in a not-God. This is not-God, that is not-God. If we equate God just with times and places and particular things or persons (even Jesus and the Gospels) then we are done for. We have imprisoned God in the little matchbox of our own minds - got you! - we are keeping God at arms length. There is the story about the well-known Christian saint, St. Paul who 'saw' God one day in a vision. He fell off his horse and found he was blind. He saw nothing - and so came to God.

How do I find God then? No one can help you do that, only open your eyes and see. All the holy ones from all the ends of the earth say in chorus - if you cannot see God in the everywhere around you then you have not got God

A salt doll wandered over hill and dale asking questions everywhere about who God is and who she was. Eventually she arrived at the edge of the great broad sea and stood there fascinated by it. "Who are you?" she said. "Come in and see," the sea smilingly replied. In she went and the deeper she went the more she dissolved until there was only very little left. Just before she finally dissolved she cried out in wonder, "Now I know the answer to both questions".

God is unchangeable Truth, says the Hindu, and is soundless, odourless, tasteless, formless, deathless, beginningless, endless.

A story about the one great lesson religions have to learn in the days that face us:- The visitor to the holy one described herself as a seeker after Truth. "One thing you must have above all else in your search for Truth", said the holy one. "I know" said the visitor, "an overwhelming passion for it". "No. The readiness at all times to admit you may be wrong".

I pray God to rid me of God.

<u>Christmas 2 - It's Christmas again....so Hello Sunshine!</u>

It's Iwanna time again. It's the skidding, skating, ice-whizzing, down hill slalom ride into the Christmas Day snowdrift. Zonk. We are besieged with Iwannas. Iwanna new mountain bike, Iwanna complete set of... Iwanna duo-axial, media-blended, double-whammy logistically synthesised computer Scoreboard (well, Elaine has one).

Iwanna make their dreams come true, Iwanna make my dreams come true, Iwanna white Christmas, Iwanna score at Christmas, Iwanna get p----d, Iwanna opt out, Iwanna have him come home, Iwanna get it right this time, Iwanna bit of peace and quiet.

Father Christmas with his oh so easy market designed question, "What do you want for Christmas?" has a lot to answer for.

Hey, Jesus baby! hello sunshine. What are you doing lying there all simple with your straightlookingout eyes? I almost didn't notice you tucked away in that crib-set under the tree. Gotta present for me then, apart from the pleasure of your company? And tell me, why are you so ordinary just like any other baby?

Jesus baby. That's it, show and tell. Sitting here godspotting, Iwanna give you, the reader, the best Christmas present I can possibly give you. And I find it's the same present I gave you last Christmas, just dressed up in different wrapping paper - no, not I hope another pair of ecclesiastical socks.

It's Jesus baby. It's hello sunshine and it's ordinary everyday. That's the pressie. My Buddhist friends have a fine way of telling it. Oh heavens, what can Buddhists possibly have to say about Christmas presents? Well listen, this is how they say it. They call it The View.

Imagine a radiant cloudless blue sky day. Then take the picture inside yourself, take it deep, deep within. For it is who you are, far below all the Iwannas, the anxieties and griefs, the hopes and fears of all the years. These are like clouds, sometimes grey, dark and threatening perhaps. Sometimes the sky seems to be so full of cloud that there looks to be nothing else. But you know, when you stop to think, that behind is the blue, the radiance. We know that sooner or later the clouds part, pass by, move on.

Under all the cellotaped prepackaging of daily life you are radiant life underneath. We are made like that - hello sunshine! - though it takes some believing, particularly at this time of year when the avalanching pressure is on. The Buddhist calls it the Buddha nature. The Christian calls it 'the light of Christ' though so often it is referred to as if it is not within at all but a distant light, like down below in a cottage window, and we are peering at it from far up on some black dark fellside.

But no! ordinary Jesus baby comes to show us that every human being is filled with the radiant Sun of God, this shining, and born as he is, so ordinary, alongside - not far from any one of us.

"O.K." you say, "I'd like to believe this but it sounds like an old cleric clacking on about cloud-cuckoo land. If this is the best present how do I unwrap it and begin to uncover this inner light I am supposed to have although I have to admit I do sometimes see a glimmer of it in other people; and just very, very occasionally in me?"

Well look at Jesus, you don't have to go all religious to do that. He never had much (began with a stable and straw) and didn't want much. He didn't live with a grasping clenched fist full of Iwannas and huge desires but with an open hand. He loved and let go, of anxieties about the past and fears of what the future had in store. He never even said 'Iwanna be happy', he just had compassion for the people he was born alongside, all the time, every moment; no matter what happened or other people thought. And so happiness, contentment, was always a possibility, a present there for the taking, wherever he went. Simple? Yes. Hard? Yes.

So when people looked at him, they saw not a clouded face but clear sky. The View. Truth. Love. Divine Light.

This couple already had a four year old daughter and the new baby was almost due. The four year old was pestering her mother every day – "Please can I see the baby as soon as it's born? Soonest! Please! Please!" Mother wasn't at all sure about all this, but at last gave way to the incessant pleading – "very well". So despite the doctors and nurses, within two minutes of the birth the child was brought in. She just came and looked. Some time later her mother asked her why it had been so important to be there immediately. The child said, "I wanted to see what God looked like again. I had almost forgotten".

On the first day of Christmas my true love said to me "Hello sunshine".

Silence and Stillness - The Silence Within

By now everything is frenetic again and we are back trying to do 101 things all at once, either because we choose to for we daren't stop (if I stop I'm dead, or at least feel worthless or not needed), or because work demands it. It certainly does for many, many people. Demands, pressure.

Stillness? silence, quietness? - a luxury just for the slower days of holidays already long gone? Yet an ancient monk said, "It is the madman who is breathless".

I went to a Quaker meeting recently. What happens there is that a group of people meet every week for an hour's silence together. It is a way of worship. Sometimes someone will speak for a few minutes but there is a lot of silence.

People go to Buddhist monasteries in increasing numbers because what is offered there is meeting together in a prayer of silence and stillness.

Up and down the land people are meeting together regularly in meditation groups, either religious or non-religious. The meeting strengthens people to maintain a discipline of time for stillness/silent prayer, whatever you call it, in their own private life, and make it a top priority. Sometimes in such a simple way, like turning off the telly for a half hour or saying firmly to the family – "I am going to my bedroom for my quiet time - please leave me alone". I know one lady who in a busy household everyday locked herself in the lavatory - that was her way. Some people drop into an open church. Yet others park the car.

People, all people, need stillness to balance with the activity and demands. It is not a luxury. People need withinness. To go within. Just as a plant needs roots. We know we need it from an early age.

Memories of a person when she was 4 – "I had an old trunk in the corner of the landing where I would go just to sit and think. It was called my peace corner and everyone in the family knew what it was. I went to it to be on my own".

A secondary school boy tells his mother – "If only I could sometimes get away from the noise and the energy, just somewhere quiet so I could catch up on my thoughts, then I would be alright ...."

A ten year old says, "That is my quiet place, where you can go if you're sad or annoyed. I like to go when no one is there, and there is a deathly silence, except for my breathing. Just your God, and the silence".

I sometimes think that we are battering to death the souls of our young with a million distractions which never leave them room to go inside. In all the bombardment of outside things we need to be in touch with ourselves, and our self is inside. Silence is the most important thing there is. There are no words to describe the most important things that happen in life.

No words to describe what it feels like to climb up the high fells up through the cloud into the sun for the first time. What sort of word is 'fantastic'? No words to tell how it is for the father who watches his child being born - he might faint! And the most people can find faced with a miracle of a new child lying in its mother's arms is "Ah, isn't she lovely".

No words for falling in love. No words for grief and death. C.S. Lewis, who wrote 'The Lion, the Witch and the Wardrobe' also wrote 'Shadowlands'. He says there, after the death of his wife, "I want people to be here but I don't want them to say anything".

No words to tell of the horror when the terrorist shoots to death the father in his own hallway in front of his wife and children.

No words. The real person grows out of the silence within. All true words come out of that centre. If we are used to going within, we will live through the best and the worst of times with balance. If we are not, our words are gobbledygook and we are like ships remaining forever restlessly at sea, never touching land, never finding safe harbour. Or like a house, empty of anything that would make it a home.

It is a terrible thing to lose your own soul, even if you have gained the whole world.

The business man called in on the holy man and said, "Look I'm desperately busy. Can you put the essence of religion into one paragraph for me"? "One word will do" said the holy one. "Incredible!" replied the other, "what amazing word is that?" "Silence".

RELIGION !

I hate the Church

I hate the Church. I also love it. On the rare occasions when my parents used to persuade (drag) me to church in my late teens I used literally to sweat with embarrassment as I listened to the rubbish the vicar seemed to spout every time he got up into the pulpit. I couldn't wait to get out. A few years later 'glory' poured from every orifice whenever the same man opened his mouth. Golden words. Brilliant visions. I couldn't hear enough, I couldn't wait for the next time. Strange - a mystery all right.

I hate Church for what it does to people. How it traps them, institutionalises them, labels them and shuts out those who really want to and need to get in. I hate the way Church so easily becomes a straitjacket to contain despair, does not set free at all. I hate the way Church becomes a grey drab prison of belief and the way church people can wipe off with sheer disregard whole sections of human life and have absolutely no tolerance for people of other integrities or religious belief. Will not listen, a cardinal sin. As if there were only one way, declaring war (to the kill) on all the others. I hate the way Church has damaged many good friends of mine. I hate the way some inside church people give the impression that we can work our passage to heaven by good deeds, breeding only self-righteousness, a sort of Sunday-best attitude to life.

So often Church chokes out the very essence it is supposed to stand for in the middle of society -forgiveness. Church can seem so unrelenting: sometimes it feels, 'The Inquisition is dead, long live the Inquisition'. Of course Church, like all institutions, needs order, but all the theological propositions, all the ecclesiastical formulae, all the high falutin' language? It's supposed to be so simple, not necessarily easy, but simple. Direct. Jesus in his lifetime cut through all the religious paraphernalia like a knife through butter, then, in the centuries that followed, it has all come piling back in again. Church tells you what to believe, but it neglects to teach you how to pray. It gives you a dictionary when you don't know the alphabet. It's like the railings round Buck Palace. Even the uniform, the holy robes, are bizarre (but I love dressing up!)

A friend was once vice-principal of a theological college. He used to ask students what was the most important theological or 'God-moment' in christening a child. "The sacramental pouring of the water?", one hopeful would suggest. No. "The signing with the cross?" another No. From all angles they never got the answer. "No" he would say. Then "it's the moment when as a vicar you get up from your tea to open your front door and there is someone standing there saying "I want my baby done please". How you receive that person in that moment is the God-moment. You make it or you lose it in the way you greet them".

Hey ho! for the Church is, after all, only like any other human institution, full of frailty, mistakes, ambition, abuse of power, desire to dominate, sheer ordinariness. They are all in place there as elsewhere.

Yet I'm torn apart because I love the Church with all my heart and soul and mind and strength. I would have been done for without the Church. It's not something I've earned, certainly not deserved, but without it my lifeship would have run aground years and years ago. Nearly did once or twice as it was. The faith that others have somehow passed on to me that the Jesus stuff is real, is what it's all about, has been my compass always guiding me back to my true North.

And I have met the most fantastic people. Such lovers of humankind that makes me feel very small. Huge people. Not in what they have done or in their position in life, but who they were or are. They have shown me how much love burns in the core of the universe if only I will watch and wait. My eyes have been opened to see such beautiful things amongst all the deviations of human existence. I have been able to dream such dreams so that, in the most squalid and horrific circumstances, my hope has always been lifted up and renewed. The encouragement of others has been immense - so many unsung heroes.

Why should I think now of one elderly woman I used to visit years ago, why should this memory affect me so? When I went into her front room straight off the street she was lying in a bed with the curtains drawn. She was paralysed from the neck down. Somehow there was a light around her, I can't explain it. We never exchanged more than a few words. One day, as I was standing looking into her amazing face, she said, "I'm at the beginning of a brand new adventure". Shortly after she died.

In all the wear and tear of belonging to Church, I love the story of Professor Lightfoot (what a good name) who eventually became Bishop of Durham. He was sitting with some students during a great 'do' in Durham Cathedral. The great procession was surging majestically down the nave with the gold cross held high and everyone dressed up in all sorts of finery, and the incense filling the place with holy smoke. The choir were going their ends and the organ was pounding the congregation to bits with vast music. Lightfoot turned to the student next to him and whispered "It's all fudge you know".

God's Law or Sod's Law?

There are those who say the bible is literally true. Literal interpretations of the bible are all very well but beware, they may lead you into deep trouble.

A U.S. radio personality who offers sex advice over the airwaves to people who call in, observed, "Homosexuality is an abomination according to Leviticus 18.v.22 and cannot be condoned in any circumstances".

A listener to the programme sent an open letter asking for further advice in relation to God's law based on specific bible laws.

1. 'When I burn a bull on the altar as a sacrifice I know it creates a pleasing odour for the Lord (Leviticus 1). The problem is my neighbours. They claim the odour is not pleasing to them. Should I smite them?'

2. 'I would like to sell my daughter into slavery as sanctioned in Exodus 21. v.7. In this day and age what do you think would be a fair price for her? She is 18 and attending university. Will the slave buyer continue to pay for education by law?'

3. 'I know that I am allowed no contact with a woman while she is in her period of menstrual uncleanliness (Lev. 15. vv. 19-24). The problem is, how do I tell? I have tried asking but most women take offence.'

4. 'Lev.25. v.44 states that I may indeed possess slaves, both male and female, provided they are purchased from neighbouring nations. A friend of mine claims this applies to Mexicans but not Canadians. Can you clarify? Why can't I own Canadians?'

5. 'I have a neighbour who insists on working on the Sabbath. Exodus 35. v.2 clearly states he should be put to death. Am I morally obligated to kill him myself or should this be a neighbourhood improvement project?'

6. 'Lev.21. v.20 states that I may not approach the altar of God if I have a defect in my sight. I have to admit that I wear reading glasses. Does my vision have to be 20/20 or is there some wiggle room? Would contact lenses help?'

7. 'Most of my male friends get their hair trimmed, including the hair around their temples, even though this is expressly forbidden by Lev. 11. v.27. How should they die?'

8. 'I know from Lev. 11. vv.6-8 that touching the skin of a dead pig makes me unclean, but may I still play football if I wear gloves?'

9. 'My uncle has a farm. He violates Lev. 19. v.19 by planting two different crops in the same field, as does his wife by wearing garments made of two different kinds of thread (cotton/polyester blend). He also tends to curse and blaspheme a lot. Is it really necessary that we go to all the trouble of getting the whole town together to stone them (Lev. 24.vv.10- 16)? Couldn't we just burn them to death, at a private family affair like we do with people who sleep with their in-laws.(Lev.20. v.14)?'

The letter ends:- "Since you have studied these things, I am confident you can help. Thank you again for reminding us that God's word is eternal and unchanging".

<u>How to become an atheist</u>

What is truth?

Mike Harding, that excruciating Northern comic, poet, folksinger and rambler extraordinary, tells how he became an atheist at the age of 8.

During scripture at school he had stuffed his fingers in his ears so that he couldn't hear properly and was a thousand miles away when he was asked a question about who God is. He tried to bluff his way out and got God mixed up with the rugby team - Trinity. By this time the teacher had got up to his desk and was towering over him. He had great warty knuckles and raised them over Mike's head, ready to crack on his skull. "God" - crunch – "is" - aw, sir! – "Love" - thumpin 'eck! Mike Harding: "I'm still trying to work that one out". Hitting people over the head with it never taught anyone the truth.

A friend once had a French schoolboy to stay who resolutely refused to learn any English at all. One day in her frustration she shook him in the middle of the street and said, "Pierre, I am going to teech yew ow to zpeek English eef eet eez ze last zing I du". You can lead a horse to water, but you cannot make it drink.

The Truth to me is the same as the word God. That has come to me through my general experience of being alive. But so many people turn from the word God because they have only experienced God as a bully or tyrant. 'You ought to believe this because it is good for you'. God the spoilsport. The God who is out to get you if you don't behave in a certain way. The God who tells you not to think, just have faith. Doubt is out. Each little package of doubt has a heavenly health warning. We still live in the aftermath of centuries of teaching about a Christian God who was supposed to be about love but really ruled by fear. Remember the Monty Python squelchy foot? The sort of God who stamps on his enemies. I meet so many good honest people of high integrity who had that sort of God rammed down their throats as a child as the Truth, so that when they reached mature years they walked right away, having nothing more to do with anything resembling religion.

I cannot really describe God to you at all. It will come out like a prescription or a formula. Yet I believe that in the idea of God is contained the secret of who I really am. The Truth about me and everyone else is hidden there.

But I know what Untruth is and I can tell you about that. It is lies. From the smallest self-deception to the biggest whoppers. Lies is about not facing the truth. They corrupt us in the measure that we use them. When we turn on lies easily we are miles out to sea. If you feel good because you have got away with it, that's another self-deception. We all practise deceit to some extent, and sometimes layer upon layer, so that having started off as a liar in certain situations we go farther and farther in and become more and more tangled and devious and shifty. In the middle of a web, and we are still spinning it.

I'm not talking about pathological liars. I'm talking about Mr. and Mrs. Nice who live in Ordinary Street. You and me. (Watch 'Neighbours', it's full of ordinary liars). Keeping up with the Joneses, or envy, is a way of lying to yourself. I wish I was someone else. If only, if only, if only.............

We all play parts and wear many masks, sometimes to impress, sometimes to hide away because we are afraid of what people will think of us - 'if they find out'. Mr. Good Guy, Mrs. Immaculate, the one who is always right; getting it perfect or being squeaky clean; the one who doesn't need anyone's help - the list is endless. We all play games with ourselves and with others. We are all dishonest, we are all petty thieves. Are you getting indignant or feeling insulted? Sorry, but that's a sure sign that I'm telling the truth about untruths.

The Bible has a phrase: 'The Devil(Evil) is the Father of Lies'. It also has another phrase: 'The Truth will set you free'. It is not important to God whether you believe in God or not. It is important to God that you are growing free all the time from the things that close down your spirit, your soul. If, as we recognise this about ourselves we determine to discard the garbage of Untruth, throw it out piece by piece, then each of us in our own unique way starts to discover what Truth is - and the Truth will set you free.

Dodgy

'Brilliant'! that's what I am. There's something I am absolutely
brilliant at, though I can't say I'm particularly pleased about it. But A
star grades? a doddle. 1st class degree? - inevitable. I'm very good at
making a God in my own image. I've been at it all my life so it's no
wonder really, and as soon as I realise I am doing it and knock down the
idol I have conjured up (a projection of myself) I find I'm building
another in its place. Good old Woody, indefatigable. I have only one
consolation and it's a pretty thin one - everybody else is doing the same
thing, constructing a god, something/someone to worship, out of their
own experience of life.

Crude God-making, a lot of it is I suppose pretty obvious - as, making an
idol of money, clothes, shopping, home and beauty, fitness, celebrity;
sometimes obsessions to which much of life is sacrificed. Usually
things you can see, touch, hold in the here and now, achievements,
career, etc., you know most of the stuff I guess.

But this is why the Bible (or any scripture) is so dodgy really if it's
taken as absolutely, literally true. It's all written by people who in their
own lives have had an overwhelming and widely varied experience of
something/someone beyond everything we know, of the mystery we all
live within. And are trying to express in human terms what is
inexpressible. People 'reaching for the stars', and of course each time
they/we try to do it, we dilute it, we get it only partly right. The Bible
is full of such half-truths -a God pleased with the sacrifice of human
life; made in an image (a sacred stone, a calf)of gold, silver, wood,
captured and worshipped as the real presence; an angry God, a God of
vengeance, a God on our side then not on our side. The Bible is shot
through with different versions of the same event, just like newspapers.
Right at the very beginning, for example, there are two different
accounts of how men and women came into being.

The writings about Jesus are the same. One gospel uses events and miracle stories in a different way from another or leaves some out as not all that important, the same difference as say between the Daily Mail and The Guardian or News of the World. Horses for courses, written for different people in different places at different times, (the gospels are not biographies). I'm glad people have wrestled like this all down the ages, without them I would have been hung out to dry a long time ago. I don't blame them or myself for trying. But each picture of God, whether inside or outside scripture, is only a signpost, not the final writing on the wall.

Our worst idols are our certainties. Taking the Daily Mail or The Guardian as 'gospel truth' (as they say!). Don't get stuck, impaled on certainties. 'I believe' does not mean 'I am certain', it means 'I have faith that..........' Keep reaching for the stars with always the readiness to admit that you know only in part. And you may be wrong. That's the best way to demolish idols.

Second-Hand Sin

Fancy a bit of Original Sin, how about it? Thing is, I don't believe in it whatever the preachers say. You might as well say we're all damn well damned from the start. I believe in Original Blessing. It's all good when it goes into the mixer, even though it may come out differently. If you look at the first few verses of the bible, which after all is a fat and important book, it's all there. Let there be light! - and God saw (we saw) that it was good. Seeds, plants, meteors and showers of light in the heavens and a great big sun, and water teeming with living creatures and sea-beasts, and cattle and creeping things and wild animals - God saw (we saw) that it was very good.

Finally human beings that were blessed to be fruitful and multiply - all very good. Somebody wrote these first verses from his experience and wonder, his astonished amazement. He believes everything in its origin, in the beginning, is very good. We did not intend to breed mad cows.

But I do believe in secondhand sin, handed down. We all share in it. Often with the best intentions. This is what I mean. Sooner or later, usually sooner, everyone experiences rejection. Comes the day, quite early, when baby newborn does not have his needs met when they need to be met. I'm hungry, the food isn't coming. Yell. Mother sleeps on, weary and weeping with unexpected demands, whilst the man who was supposed to be on hand to help as they agreed and wanted, has had to work away. Or child cries out in pain and parents think it's having them on -or a neighbour calls and interrupts things "Oh! he knows what he wants that one, he just wants attention". Of course he bloody well does!

Later when a child has a tantrum on the supermarket floor because he can't sort out his moods and feelings and words, he gets shaken and belted then and there! Once, just as the priest was holding aloft the bread and the wine, consecrating the holy moment, I saw mother reach out and give her noisy little angel a right cracker – "Lord God Almighty, Heaven and Earth are full of your glory" - Bam! Or the action-packed tiny human dynamo who has just thrown her cooking set at the television, is banished. Secondhand sin. All of it. Nobody's fault much of the time. Often done with the best intentions. Secondhand sin is the experience of rejection. Of being made to feel beyond the pale, unacceptable because of what I did or did not do or say. Filling my nappy just once too often. First experience with f and s words. At this moment I do not belong. Ask any adult who was a middle child what it feels like to be squeezed out; the injustice of not having the attention you felt was due to you and clearly seemed to be given to numbers 1 and 3.

We tough out most of these things. Some of us are tougher than others. Also from time to time we can experience in the family and in the world a sense of failure and defeat, of being despised out of all proportion to the event. Something so small, yet it rankles for ever, embedded like a bullet in the brain. Or the punishment did not fit the crime. Innocent, we had to take the blame. You could almost call all this hard porn. It's the stuff of distortion, nightmare, betrayal, the seeds of holocaust. Because this is how we were treated, it can be how we learn to treat others - by rubbishing them, cutting them out, 'you don't fit here'. I don't need to spell it out any more. We have all developed our own way of killing people stone dead with a look, a word, some (or most) of the time. Rejection is what we have all experienced, an infection that got into the blood stream early.

For some of us, a small error towards us early on can lead to a huge gap in the way we are with people later on. Like an error in map-reading. A fraction of a degree out on a compass and you can land up miles away on the other side of the fell with a long walk home, or worse, be completely lost; secondhand sin, the experience of rejection. Cain killed his brother because he thought, rightly or wrongly, that he was getting more favourable treatment. The mark of Cain is on us all. Sin makes people feel excluded. Community (communion), belonging together, being interdependent, is health. It is the staff of life. It is right. It is what we are made for. I am writing this on World Aids Day.

The holy community is not a church particularly, or synagogue, or mosque, or monastery. It is any community, or man or woman, who comes up and says, "Come in my dear, you are the very one we have been looking for".

Spiritual Press Ups

Have you ever tried training a puppy? You sit down and say "Stay" and it runs away. You sit it down again and it runs away again. Over and over again. Sometimes it will jump up, run off and pee in a corner or make some other mess. You can get quite frustrated and may want to beat the daylights out of it but that doesn't help if you want it to be your friend. With you. On your side, not cowering or growling angry. Gradually, gradually, is the way.

Spiritual practice, training, is just like this. We keep running off and making bigger messes. We keep peeing in the eye of God - what a pretty picture - well, we do. Why bother with spiritual practice? Because we are worth it: it does lead the way to a sense of fulfilment, of being right with the world, some happiness and contentment. If you really want to practise, spiritually to train yourself, here are three simply things to keep doing. Simple does not mean easy: it is simple enough to sit a puppy down, it's another matter to get it to stay.

Practise Acceptance of yourself and others. We are not to achieve any Olympic standard. We cannot. We are not looking for perfection. There is none in our spiritual life, thank God. Perfectionism generates 'holier-than-thous', hatreds, real inquisitions. If we strive for perfection in ourselves or anybody else, we shall always end up disappointed. Too many marriages are ruined because one partner thought the other was the perfect answer to all their needs and hopes and put them on a pedestal. We are not seeking to say "I've made it", achieving some fantasy level of goodness.

We are never going to be particularly good at loving, we are only going to get it right part of the time, that's the way of things. We shall, with practice, learn to recognise some of our mistakes and avoid them, growing en route in courage to recognise the difficulties we face in loving ourselves and others and cultivate compassion. Self-forgiveness is this first step. It's not falling in the mud that matters it's the not getting up. "The test of a good life is not how you live in good times but how you manage in bad times" (Peter Gomes). And yes! Bit by bit we shall become brighter, fitter, more loving, more loveable - the goal of life.

So I'm not suggesting you take up some grim, self punishing routines, a sour-faced duty. We need to learn to laugh at ourselves, gently and generously, otherwise we shall become too serious and tightlipped. Down the generations the Church has often been at fault in making it seem that spiritual practice is to do with grinding down the self, putting the screws on - 'go on- be miserable'. We shall get fed up. We shall go so long and find ourselves back at the beginning it seems. We shall stop. And we can start again - good dog!

Practise Kindness. What we have to practise doing is creating distance between our thoughts/feelings and our actions. If we can start to act kindness no matter what's going on inside this can help us to think (to be) kindness. How we start to behave in ordinary life transforms how we are in spirit. So no harsh impositions, just try breaking some lifetime mind sets. Mrs. A. had always hated Mr. B.. Something about him made her shiver. The sideways look in his eyes? His slouchy walk? In any case he was a grumpy old sod, never a good word to anyone. Then, he could no longer walk to the Pensioners' Luncheon Club, the cheap meal, the only place he ever went. So, every week Mrs.A began to phone him and take him in her car. And back after. That's all. And when he died, she went to his funeral with the other two people. Even just saying hello to someone you've always ignored is a huge step for mankind.

And *Practise Patience.* You have often heard it said "I've no patience, I'm not that kind of person". Oh no! you can grow patience, you just have to be patient! You can learn not to snap back, not to retaliate. You can learn not to say the first thing that comes into your mouth, not always to follow your anger and your resentment. You can learn to count, not to 10 but to 20. Not to pass judgement. "If you ask me what sin is, I know instantly with reference to myself. I haven't the slightest idea with reference to anyone else". (Martin Buber).

An R.A.F. senior officer had just returned from a stress-management course. He was standing in a supermarket queue with just a couple of items. Ahead at the checkout a woman held a baby and she and the woman on the till were goo-ing over it, just taking their time. He was

143

in a hurry. He could feel his impatience rising, his anger at being kept waiting. Remembering the course, he sought to keep calm, talk himself down quietly and wait; so that when he came to pay he was even able to say, albeit grudgingly, "That was a fine baby". "Yes" the woman replied, "he's my son. You see my husband was a pilot and he was killed last year in an air exercise so now I have to have a job. My mother brings my boy in every day so that I can just say "hello" to him for a few minutes".

Daily spiritual practice leads to not forgetting - to accept yourself as an ordinary, lovely, human being; to be kind; and to be patient.

Vulnerable

Sometimes you have to turn things upside-down to get them the right way-up. Like the word 'vulnerable' (weak), it always seems to be cropping up these days. Then the word 'strong'. But what is 'strong'?

Well, I saw a really 'strong' man recently. He was solid, no-neck Cumbrian, with a giant chest, built like a front-row forward. That marvellous crunch physique. But no, he wasn't lifting up the front of a car with his left hand. With his right hand he was holding the hand of his grown-up bulky daughter, disabled in body and mind, and quietly guiding her through a waiting room full of people to see a doctor. You saw years and years in that man of a guiding, guarding father, with all the heartbreaks and yes, the times also of really living. So vulnerable he was with such gentle strength.

'Strong' leaders? Why can't politicians see that they would gain trust and respect and be more listened to if they were publicly 'vulnerable' on occasions, admitting mistakes, miscalculations, such as every other human being has, instead of trying to remain 'strong'? "Sorry? My fault? -not in my lifetime! What I did was within the rules" - we know that one! What happens to you when you arrive politically or economically at the places of high power?

But it seems most of us will do anything rather than let our defences down. We will lie, cheat, swear blind, shout loud, or just say nothing, wield the big stick, anything to prevent others from seeing our fault lines (our warm frailties).

A Catholic priest recently went incognito into a most poor decaying working-class area, high unemployment, with high dependency on social services. He really hadn't a clue about setting up a flat, even how to deal with gas/electricity meters. He felt helpless, realising how much his feeling 'strong' had depended on his role and achievements. He was immediately taken in hand by these most vulnerable people who knew the ropes. You could see in their facelines, he said, the hardness of life, yet they all rallied round and were glad to do so. He was astonished.... "so many interruptions in the name of a cup of tea or coffee...!"

Powerless, utterly vulnerable, these same people mistrusted everyone in authority with any power, including inevitably the Church, because they felt either resented or patronised, not welcome. Yet out of their weakness they gave one another the strength to find some light in the day. Here the priest says, I was discovering what community, what real living was all about: 'strong' because they knew how vulnerable they were and shared it.

These are no <u>more</u> feckless or spongers than the rest of us higher up the scale, richer, better fed, who also practice playing the system from time to time. We have so much to learn, sitting as we do in our comfortable places. And you will have noticed how people who care for others are so often people who were cared for themselves in times of great need - widows, desperate sickness, refugees, the violently abused – "my child died and I'm doing this because I don't want others to go through..." These lovely lines from a psalm (84):- 'who trudging through the plains of misery/find in them an unexpected spring/a well from deep below the barren ground/and the pools are filled with water./ They become springs of healing for others/ reservoirs of compassion to those who are bruised/ strengthened themselves they give courage to others'.

It is one of the bible saints, Paul, who says "it is when I am weak that I am strong". It is the vulnerable who will ultimately inherit the earth because in the end they are the ones who are really strong. Welcome to the real, right-way-up world.

INTERLUDE - The Church Notice Board!

- Don't let worry kill you. Let the Church help.

- Thursday night - Potluck Supper. Prayer and medication to follow.

- Remember in prayer the many who are sick of our church and community.

- For those of you who have children and don't know it, we have a nursery downstairs.

- The rosebud on the altar this morning is to announce the birth of David Alan Belzer, the sin of Rev. and Mrs. Julius Belzer.

- This afternoon there will be a meeting in the south and north ends of the church. Children will be baptized at both ends.

- Tuesday at 4p.m. there will be an ice cream social. All ladies giving milk will please come early.

- Thursday at 5p.m. there will be a meeting of the Little Mothers Club. All wishing to become Little Mothers, please see the minister.

- This being Easter Sunday, we will ask Mrs. Lewis to come forward and lay an egg on the altar.

- The service will close with 'Little Drops of Water'. One of the ladies will start (quietly) and the rest of the congregation will join in.

- The ladies of the church have cast off clothing of every kind and they may be seen in the church basement on Friday.

- A bean supper will be held on Tuesday evening in the church hall. Music will follow.

- Weight Watchers will meet at 7p.m. at the First Presbyterian Church. Please use large double door at the side entrance.

- The 1991 Spring Council Retreat will be hell May 10th to 11th.

- Pastor is on vacation. Massages can be given to church secretary.

- 8 new choir robes are currently needed, due to the addition of several new members and to the deterioration of some older ones.

- Mrs. Johnson will be entering the hospital this week for testes.

- The Senior Choir invites any member of the congregation who enjoys sinning to join the choir.

- Please join us as we show our support for Amy and Alan who are preparing for the girth of their first child.

- The Associate Minister unveiled the church's new tithing campaign slogan last Sunday - **'I Upped My Pledge - Up Yours'.**

Crossroads

A crossroads is a place where all roads meet. Come together. Imagine people walking in from each direction. They all meet together at the crossroads. Often in the olden days, there would be an inn there, a vitally important place where people would stop off. As dark gathered there would be lights on, the door would be open with welcome, and people coming from the four corners would stop for rest, refreshment, sleep, exchanging news. Stranger would meet stranger. Friendships would form.

A word for a 'solitary' person in Russia also means an 'inn' - a place where travelling alone and perhaps loneliness can be left on the doorstep.

People are supposed to be crossroads. We are meant to be gathering places where others may meet and find welcome, consolation, easement from hardship and suffering (a sorrow shared is a sorrow halved), laughter, fun. Someone to listen to their story and who will accept ours. It is what each person in their heart is supposed to be, though we fall short; a meeting place for others. We are born out of a meeting (man with woman, egg with sperm) and without meetings happening again and again, moment after moment, in our lives, we die. We shrivel and die (though we may not actually be breath-dead).

People with faith in the goodness of meeting and getting to know others see this clearly. Are they there, perhaps, to show the way? Not necessarily people of religion but people of faith. Religion so often puts fences around faith, creates divisions, erects barriers. Establishes road-blocks. 'When the red light shows, stop here!' Puts up diversion signs so that we never meet people coming in the opposite direction. There's a big hole in the road dug by Religions.

Religions are just meant to be signposts to the kingdom within, posting the way towards the crossroads. The kingdom within can only be revealed by people meeting. People of faith who are also religious know this and seek to unbar the way to the inn where all roads meet. They are not popular. They are often called heretics, unbelievers, and life for them can never be comfortable. For they are prepared to meet those coming from very different directions who may speak differently, act and look very different. As different as an innocent-eyed wolf. Do

148

you know the story of such a wolf?

Once upon a time there was a lonely wolf lonelier than the angels.

He happened to come to a village. He fell in love with the first house he saw. Already he loved its walls, the caresses of its bricklayers. But the windows stopped him. In the room sat people. Apart from God nobody ever found them so beautiful as this child-like beast. So at night he went into the house. He stopped in the middle of the room and never moved from there anymore. He stood all through the night with wide eyes, And on into the morning when he was beaten to death.

The people who beat the wolf to death were the people behind the safe walls of the house. Not the people of faith. Jesus, though a man of his religion, who honoured it and loved it, was also a man of faith who went beyond it. A Jew amongst Jews but also a Jew amongst Palestinians and others. For him God was more 'here' than 'there'. He lived God out in the heart of his life and there was no division between gospel and life. Every moment a meeting. Always remaining faithful to the first moments of conception (whatever they were for him those first moments of meeting) and going on with every stride to make new meetings, new communions amongst people, creating spaces between where there were no barriers. Jesus always a crossroads. Anyone could arrive, just anyone.

So they said, the religious with no faith, "since that's how he sees himself and how he acts, we'll make him a crossroads signpost and put him on it". Which they did. His hands and feet beaten into it. I have to say that any religion would have done the same, they have done just the same many times since. You can only go so far with Religions.

"We're very ecumenical these days" the speaker said. "On Good Friday (the day Jesus was beaten to death) in addition to our own services, we come together in an act of witness and worship for all the churches". Voice from the crowd "Do you say in addition to or replacing them, instead of?" Speaker – "Oh in addition to. We did our own thing first". Voice – "Ah me! Another Good Friday without any sacrifices".

Funny - we wear the ornamental cross around our necks or in our ears without for a moment thinking what sort of crossroads it is inviting us to be.

Forgive

The sign of the cross, a Christian sign. Christianity takes a lot of bashing these days, often with a sneer of contempt, only a fool would go along with that. So it is important to be very clear about this one central thing, the sign of the cross on which a man hung and died, a very public lynching, a very public humiliation. The essential difference between Christianity and all other religions is that the God of the Christian suffers. To a Muslim (and a Jew) it is inconceivable that God should suffer, a blasphemy. As one Muslim said to a bishop "I could never respect a God who allowed men to treat him like that".

The sign of the Cross. That is where Christians stand no matter how foolish it may seem. And here's a bit more foolishness. God suffers willingly, Jesus suffers willingly, because God forgives. Unconditionally. Forgiveness is as much part of Jesus as two arms and legs are to every human being. It's there from the start, it's how he looks out on the world. Forgiveness, he reveals in his living and dying, is natural to being alive. It is something we experience again and again in the face, in the actions of any child at the beginning of its life; it comes back again and again with unconditional trust, not really noticing our tantrums and mistakes. This is how we were. But the child too soon has it knocked out of him one way or another: she becomes a victim who has to defend herself, shield herself by being over against others; and forgiveness becomes something we only offer sometimes to some people, usually just those whom we feel to be on our side.

Not so with Jesus. Jesus never loses that childlikeness, the childlikeness of God. He looks into every mortal soul with the eyes of continuing forgiveness, even those whose ways he condemns. That's why he's so often such hard company because he immediately penetrates our pettiness and hypocrisy, the way we grade ourselves over against others, and jockey for position. When we are hardhearted, reject and condemn, or do not even notice, God suffers because of our hardness of heart, but the idea that we can wound God, that God can be so 'soft', such a fool, is anathema to many. What a preposterous notion! Sometimes our lack of forgiveness accuses us so deeply that we cannot bear it and turn away to find a scapegoat, someone else to blame and that we can take it out on.

That's what happened to Jesus. He's open, not closed, a soft touch we think. His presence, his words, his complete integrity pierces like the sharpest knife through the selfish armour of power, prestige and position. He exposes in our inner self how far we are from the truth about really being alive. We are never really alive if we live at the expense of others, that's why he's so hard to take. So the sign of the cross. Crucify him. This God suffers now, as then: such foolishness, such cloud cuckoo land, 'they' say.

Forgiveness oils the machinery of the world, forgiveness is the opportunity to start again. That's why Christians attract suffering and the taunt of foolishness and will always do so, because instead of being over-against they will go on standing shoulder to shoulder with those who cannot forgive, together with the victims and oppressed of this world. To practice forgiveness is to invite hurt and much suffering and ridicule, but this volunteering to suffer in this way is why people in many parts of the world are flooding to Christian things: the idea of a God who is always on their side and suffers with them is new. Ridiculous! Marvellous!

The sign of the cross. Jesus dies on the cross because he forgives. That's why Christians believe he is raised from the dead and can talk about him in the present tense, because he goes on forgiving on both sides of death. In Jesus, God lays all his cards on the table. So if you want to be as God in this world, this is where you begin and end - with forgiveness.

Loss of Faith

Now this is weird. You are going to read this at the beginning of August but here I am feeling compelled to start on 8th May. What will the August weather be like because these May days, are amazing; constant sunlight, blue, blue in the sky all the day, the lightest of warm breezes; gardens, hedgerows everywhere suddenly on blossom-alert, all into full green. And here I am like you, transfixed with horror (again) at the Burmese tsunami, whole villages buried in sand, towns swept away, the dead hanging in trees............need I go on? And then days after, a massive earthquake at Chechuan in China, with whole schools and student halls of residence buried. And so it's August, and perhaps apart from the update of third or fourth item news flashes, we have 'moved on', emotionally anyway, from Burma and China.

Why 8th May? Because in the Church of England this is St. Julian's Day, who, through her own terrible sufferings nearly to death, and the appalling and bewildering sufferings of her own times (14th century), had visions that the Love which for her is God and Jesus is ever good and will never fail.............She saw, in one vision, in the palm of her hand a hazelnut and thought "it is all that is made......I thought it might have crumbled to nothing, it was so small". And the thought came "it lasts and ever shall because God loves it". Then, she also said "All shall be well/and all shall be well/and all manner of things shall be well".

Throw up against this the vast cynicism about anything religious in our down-mouthed nation. Don't ask me to explain the suffering conundrum of her sayings in any other terms than her faith. And we have lost faith. Faith in what has gone before. Faith in ourselves, faith in our world and faith in the whole process of Creation of which we are an intimate and integral part. We have become unhealthily self-absorbed and have lost the larger picture.

We need to distinguish again, between <u>optimism</u> and <u>hope.</u>

Optimism is the idea that things will get better, we shall see results, in our lifetimes. Hope is a faith in simple loving; that far beyond our lifetimes and our understanding, "all shall be well".

Loving-kindness will rule: hey! I have friends who plant oak trees for the world to come. Why does not 'God' step in? Because 'God' is already well in, in our hearts, waiting to be part of our every breath, every movement, and beyond, beyond. God will not twist our arms. But will not fail us.

Here's a small thing. A friend was having a bad day at Heathrow Airport. Where else! He had missed his boarding call to Mexico by 5 minutes and was shut out by the computer. Phone Mexico, let them know. He discovers his small palm-top computer is flat. He goes to a mobile-phone shop to see if they sell chargers. "No", she says. But then she says – "we have some equipment on charge and I could put your palm-top in with them," "I was astonished" he said, "such a simple kindness". He goes off for food, returns later, half expecting his palm-top might have been pinched. "Oh no!" she says "I kept my eye on it".

It is through such incessant simple acts of kindness repeated trillions of times each day in and beyond our lifetimes, by us and others, all over the world, that "all shall be well". Have faith in the process which is evolving; and note perhaps the simple acts of loving-kindness going on, quite unselfconsciously, through you and all around you.

Note:- The Julian Shrine, which was and is a place of pilgrimage for people from all over the world, is at:

St. Julian's Church, All Hallows, Rouen Road., Norwich, NR1 1QT just 1/2 mile from the cathedral.
Telephone:01603-767380
www.julianofnorwich.org

<u>Beyond Religions</u>

Oh no! not Muslims again? Well, why not, it's the Big (God) Issue innit? So - the word got around that the Muslim holy man was in town. Everyone flocked to the town square to hear him offer some words of encouragement in the practice of their religion and faith. Eventually he came out with a pail of water in one hand and a flaming torch in the other. "The water", he said, "is to quench the fires of Hell, and the torch is to set fire to Paradise". With that he disappeared.

The story was told by a Muslim to a large gathering of Christians and Muslims who met at York University a year or two back to pray together, talk together and discover friendships - the point of the story being that all religions must be prepared to let go of teachings that they may have previously held dear, like ideas about Heaven and Hell.

God, it was said, is in vast denial by most of Western Europe, even though 'God' is at the heart of all our history. But God in one form or another is always in the way, in front of us like a road-block, inescapable in the history of time, there from the beginning, unmissable, always present in the yearnings of humankind. We have to put 'God' back at the centre of human life and practice once more. The 'breath of God' is in every human heart and wants us, always, to come back home.

The religious do all sorts of things with the notion of God and we get stuck in doctrines and interpretations as if they were fixed for all time. The ongoing task of religion is to move us on to a different place beyond religions. 'Religion' is what you think you know about God, yet God is beyond all we know, always, beyond even the whole mystery of the universe. Religion is supposed to move us eventually into the empty space beyond all we know, the stillness of the Great Unknown, that silent place beyond our words to describe; which we all come to (the greatest wordless space is death). 'Good God!' is a fine phrase. God is only good, nothing else; good as we interpret the best of human behaviour in the practice of justice and equality, and care for each other. The only competition that should be shown amongst religions is to have the humility to compete with one another in acts of goodness and loving kindness.

We are to look for unity amongst religions but not confusion; confusion would be a desperate dilution of all our beliefs to a worthless minimum. Unity means not two, yet not one, we remain unique yet inseparable, interdependent. So we need real difference where it matters but not division. At present we are allowing our differences bitterly to divide us.

At York it was Muslims talking with Christians and agreeing, but what about the Muslim violence across the world? A true Muslim will tell you that Muslims will only respond with violence if violence is first practised against them, and then only if there is injustice to other human beings (same as the Christian 'just war' example. Britain in 1939 after the Nazi invasion of Poland).

Also then, a Christian story about where religions should be going. Jesus meets a Samaritan woman at a well at midday. To a Jew (Jesus) she is doubly to be despised. First she is a Samaritan, an alien, unapproachable. Also she is a woman drawing water from the well at the heat of the day where respectable women would come in the cool of the evening. Clearly an outcast, a prostitute. Jesus asks her to draw water for him. "Our fathers," she says, "worshipped on this mountain while you say that Jerusalem is the place where we ought to worship". Jesus replies, "The hour will come - in fact it is here already - when true worshippers will worship the Father in spirit and truth: this is the kind of worshipper the Father wants. God is spirit and those who worship must worship in spirit and truth". (St John's Gospel. Chapter 4)

Silence and Stillness – Meditation 1

Meditation. I meditate. I teach meditation. Silent prayer, contemplation, call it what you will. Specifically Christian Meditation. "Aha!" they tap their noses knowingly, "that's where he gets all his queer ideas about God. No wonder! It's all this Eastern stuff."

When I mention meditation, those who most frequently turn away sharply and say not today thank you (or any day) are churches and clergy. Very resistant the Church is to meditation. No time for it as a rule. And this is not simply my experience, it happens to people who practise Christian meditation up and down the country whenever they mention it.

Yet 'hear ye, hear ye!'. Most of you who read this will admit that a Pope has his problems. You may find some of the teachings he stands for and pronounce about very difficult. But this is what he had to say a few recent years ago, He stresses the 'duty of Christians now to draw from this rich heritage (of India) the elements compatible with their faith' and he says 'that the Church of the future will judge herself enriched by all that comes from today's engagement with Eastern cultures and will find in this inheritance fresh clues for fruitful dialogue with the cultures which will emerge as humanity moves into the future'.

And as long ago as 1968 the Church of England, through its Lambeth Conference said, 'The Church should pay more attention to the development of that capacity for silent prayer which exists in all her members. In this field we have much to learn from the approach of oriental religions to silence'.

A final word from one of the great Archbishops of Canterbury in our lifetime, Archbishop Michael Ramsey – "A Church which starves itself and its members in the contemplative life ('meditation' my word) deserves whatever spiritual leanness it may experience."

Meditation these days comes in through many doors. You don't have to believe in God or in anything except yourself. But it is the same whichever door you come through - whether humanist at one end or Christian at the other. It is a neutral discipline which you apply to your particular way of looking at life. Meditation is like a candle. Candles are big business used in all sorts of ways for all sorts of celebrations, worship, special events. Lighting scented candles around yourself as you languish exotically in your bathtub are just all the rage. We do not prohibit the use of candles in Church just because others use them in other ways. Christians use them and attach to them their own particular meanings drawn from the Church's traditions ('Christ the light of the world, etc.') The same for meditation.

'Meditation' actually means 'standing in the middle of', so it is about coming into the middle of your own self, your own centre and discovering there the resources to ease stress, anxiety, bring peace, assist change, renew faith. So you can meditate to relieve your stress in your job (some workplaces now have meditation rooms), aim for a more healthy lifestyle, get in touch with your vibrations and relax, etc. Meditation is centred on the human experience that understanding yourself is the bedrock of all other certainties; and if you are running away from yourself you are running away from everything else.

For the Christian, it is then a common, neutral discipline which you apply to Christian things. 'The Kingdom of Heaven is within you' is one of Jesus' sayings and you must seek it there. It will not arrive from outside unless you first discover it on the inside.

The Christian does not meditate first and foremost to feel better (though this may certainly happen) but as an act of faith in God's way, in Christ. Buddhists do the same with their faith in the Buddhist way, so do Hindus with their own non-Christian insights. Meditation is a common denominator, each using it in our own way. There's nothing to be afraid of.

It is simple (which is why I do it and teach it), and it is a discipline (which is why I need it). It is not for special people, it is for everybody. We all need silence, we all have it within us. The hectic habby-dashy, express delivery world in which we live keeps driving us past the stop where we need to get off. We need to get off.

Silence and Stillness – Mediation 2

How do you do this simple thing? I meditate in this way:- decide a time, say 10 minutes, and make a point of finding somewhere each day where you will stop and just be still, doing absolutely nothing. That's the discipline. Try to make sure you are comfortable and relaxed, sitting, lying down, kneeling, whatever. It will not always be possible for it to be the same part of the day everyday. During that time, choose a word or phrase that has sacred meaning, religious or otherwise according to your tradition and understanding. Then say it quietly to yourself, hang on to it, repeat it, refocus on it when it gets lost, for all that time. It's not hypnosis, just keeping a sense of direction like a compass pointing you again to your true North.

Many people who practise meditation like this find that after a while, when they miss doing it, they really miss it. They often seek to extend the time - 20 to 30 minutes is thought to be ideal. But be gentle with yourself. Go slowly.

It is simple and I have to say that it also takes courage. A discipline always requires some courage. Courage because little by little it brings us face to face with the games of let's pretend we play with ourselves and other people. It shows me how shallow and superficial I can be and I don't like that. But facing these things helps us to loosen their hold on us and go through them. Though they come and come again, say hello to them and then say goodbye.

It's a bit like restoring a lovely old painting - an old master. Cleaning off the grime is painstaking, it is work, but bit by bit the beauty and harmony and balance of the original colours -which you are, this is your truth - begin to be restored.

To rediscover in the silence that we are after all made in the image of goodness. Much easier, in the short run, to chase on and do something else, anything rather than be still. Easier, is it though, in the long run, to stay with the faded devilish bits of ourselves (better the devil you know) than to uncover the real glory of the original?

GROWING UP

Dr. Who and You

Harvest-home? Ears of golden corn? All is safely gathered in? You must be joking. For some families the only harvest coming home is their dead, stabbed young, (police amnesties 'harvest' thousands of knives each time, yes?) Two more this very morning. About a third of our young carry knives at some time or another. To ask "what are they up to?" is to ask the wrong question. Rather, what are we up to? For I am, you are, Mack the Knife. The young are only living out what they notice, how much of the world chooses or is forced to live. Copy-cat lives. The knife is in your hand. In mine. They are not aliens from another planet. They are our young.

Many people live their working lives on a knife-edge of short-term contracts or huge swinging market uncertainties, with early cut-off points. Cut your losses, move on. We have grown to become wasters of people: we describe individuals as 'wasted space', and the culture we are caught up in and go along with is forever stabbing people in the back (and front), from the smallest gesture to the most cunning political manoeuvres, in work, in boardrooms, in constituency parties. Supermarkets - cut price: cut-throat competition. Celebrities cut each other out, stab with words and gestures. Here's a favourite cut - the bouncing young man or woman zooms into a disabled parking space, bawls out a sod-off at any limping protest and disappears (or "I'll only be a minute!!") We have learnt to disrespect one another so well in recent years.

Of course there's something wrong with us! Do we not belong to a human race that in the last century killed over 100 million people? Violence is endemic. The pollution of the planet is simply an outward sign of an inward pollution. It is amazing there are so many brilliant young.

We don't need any more inspectorates haranguing us about what to do. We know. We have just lost our nerve, lost courage, become moo-moo, baa-baa, going with the herd. Each of us has to begin again (and again and again, for we make many mistakes) doing what we can to disarm our own corner of the universe though that may seem insignificant in the order of things. We are caught up in a world-wide spiritual dis-ease. In order to face the violence 'out there', we have to face the violence in ourselves. Drop the knife. Quietly to seek always to value the other person (especially the young) equally in all circumstances, as we wish always to be valued. Learn to disarm by the words and gestures we use, and more often by the words and gestures we do not use, so that they become a forbidden vocabulary, forbidden body-language. It's a discipline, of course it is. It is hard, of course it is, to go against the herd. It is our fears which infect our young.

Want a non-religious role model? Dr. Who shows the way. When a soldier shoots to kill Dr. Who's newly-discovered daughter, he rushes over to the soldier, holds a gun to his head with the trigger cocked for a long time; but then, finally, says, tremblingly "Remember, I am the one who would not – ever". And walks away.

Karma

Karma is not what you get at an Indian restaurant, the chef's special.

When I was working in S.E. Lancashire the police phoned late one winter's night to say that they were at the home of a certain man, let's call him Geoffrey Dodd. He'd asked for me. I knew him quite well, I had baptised the latest baby. When I got there, the front door was wide open, the light flooding onto the street, and there he was standing at the bottom of the stairs. He'd beaten up his wife. With tears streaming down his face he pointed to his five year old son standing at the top of the stairs, also weeping in utter bewilderment. Geoffrey said, "I remember when I was just his age standing at the top of our stairs when my dad beat up my mum and saying to myself this will never happen to me". That's Karma.

In South Africa violence was systematically practised by whites upon blacks for generations, it was government policy – 'treat them like animals, they are only just down from the trees'. Now in the 'liberated' South Africa violence is huge, black upon white, black upon black. There is no work, no money. Crime, treating others as if they didn't exist as human beings, is the only way for many without hope. That is Karma.

Those who sexually abuse children are usually those who were themselves abused as children. Karma.

I was having a health check once. The nurse said, "Any history of heart disease in your family?" "No." "Stroke?" "No." "It's easy to see you didn't grow up in West Cumbria". That is part of the Karma of the West Coast.

Karma is the endless round of human suffering. It is often hard to escape the consequences of lives that were lived before we were born. The bible talks about the sins of the fathers being visited upon the children right through to the third and fourth generations - that is what it means. The evil or good we do lives after us. We are often helpless in the grip of things that happened before we were born and can feel punished by them. 'Punished' is a word people use - what have I done to deserve this? The law of cause and effect.

The things we do have consequences. It is obvious. And they will be reincarnated in babies born after we die. And the karma of George Best, unable to cope with the full strength of his amazing gifts, as he was drawn back again into the trauma of his drinking, was one of the sporting tragedies of my lifetime. A man much more crippled than many disabled people.

Buddhists talk about the discipline of living the good life. What they mean by that is seeking to diminish suffering. Anything we do, consciously or unconsciously, which perpetuates the cycle of suffering in ourselves or others, is not the good life.

To break the endless cycles of repeated suffering is the practical goal of the living. That is living the Buddha life (or the Christ life). It is the only thing that counts; compassionate living alone frees from pain. For Buddha this has nothing to do with God. We can believe in a God if we like, and that's fine, it may help, but such a belief is meaningless if it does not come to the same point - seeking to cause suffering to cease.

These days do we have a new saint. St. Rednose, the saint of comic relief? She/he has become a major festival for the nation. Every year, all over the land, people laugh and have fun and give money freely. To do what? To break the karma of others. To lift them to a fuller life. To laugh in the face of the most terrible privations and to plant trust and hope and beauty and goodness in the good spring earth of mankind. To warm the days. To say it doesn't have to be like this for ever and ever. We refuse to allow it. Brilliant. Even those who feel stuck in their present sufferings joke defiantly, determined to release others; and in so doing start to release themselves.

Religion is to do with knowing that something is wrong and seeking to reconnect with what is tried and trusted down the ages, known in human life to be good and true. When reconnections are made people begin to see over their present horizons, they begin to get cleaned up and leave behind their old painful selves. 'Purified' is a holy word but it is a right sort of word. There's nothing wrong with applying it to you and me.

'Heaven' is what we discover being given to us when suffering has ceased. Buddhists call this state 'nirvana' which means 'cooling off' or 'going out'. They describe suffering as a flame; a person who suffers is enflamed. Nirvana is what happens when the flame is blown out, when all the cycles of karma have been broken. Call it 'blessedness', 'wholeness', 'perfect love', 'truth'. Whatever all this heaven talk is, it is beyond even 'God' because 'God' is in the end only words; our word for it. What is beyond, yet what is there for us all, is Inexpressible, Beyond words. A beyond without Karma, it is the final mystery beyond all our living.

The Archer

Sin. Been at it, have you? Who me? Yes, you. NO, sir, not me, sir! Oh, come off it, of course you have, you're doing it all the time. WE ALL ARE. Miserable sinner. How do you fancy that for a name? Make you a bit hot under the collar, or a bit red in the face? Not a particularly nice word 'sin', and certainly one we don't like to associate with ourselves. Other people, perhaps.

Well, let's be a bit cool about sin. What does it mean? In this case it's important to go back to the root of the meaning of the word. The second half of the bible, the New Testament, the Jesus bit, was originally written in Greek (what? not English, goodness me what's the world coming to), and the New Testament word for 'sin' (hamartia) is actually an archery term meaning to miss the target. Sinning is living off-target. It means not aiming - your life - in the right direction.

There's a story about the master archer. He was always saying "Aim for perfection". This got up the nose of one of his students – "Show us then, show us perfection". The master stood perfectly still for a long time with his eyes closed. He then told them to black out the great practice hall and place a target at the far end. He took his bow. In the black dark they all waited. All was utterly still. Then the swoosh of the arrow and the sound of it hitting the target. They opened the blackout and the arrow was right through the centre of the target. "Fluke" said the student. The master took a second arrow. He told the student to blindfold him and turn him round and round whilst the blackout fell in place again. Once more all became very still. Then finally the swoosh of the arrow cleaving the air a second time. They opened the blackout and the second arrow had split the first arrow in two.

That is what it means to be sinless. Perfection, the centre of the target, is to live just 'as a bee, without harming the flower its colour or scent, goes from flower to flower, collecting only the honey' - (The Dhammaparda - a Buddhist scripture). Being on target, is the point of being alive. Any situation where you do not look to each other's interest equally as at the same time you look to your own, is sin. Every person you meet is an occasion to shoot for gold.

The shock is that we are all master archers, we're made like that. We just have to become what we already are. How about this for a list of popular sins. 'Sod off' is sin. (say it or think it, it's the same). 'Couldn't care less' - is sin. Sitting on the fence - is sin. Gossip - is sin. One unkind word is sin; 'I never did anybody any harm' (you must be joking). 'No one will ever notice' - is sin. There is no such thing as private sin, one drop of water ripples the whole pool.

Would you knowingly take poison? Anger, desire and ignorance, says the Buddhist, are the three poisons. Do not accuse; judge not or you will be accused, says the Christian. All these things come out of misery, our own, and create misery in others. Miserable sinner.

'Repent, the Kingdom of Heaven is at hand' glares the billboard in lurid dayglo. It sounds like a doom watch cry. 'Repent' usually means change direction, you are looking in the wrong place. The real target is just at hand, not very far away at all. 'Repent' is the whisper of a lover, not the bellow of a jail-keeper; telling us what we want to know most of all, that the kingdom of heaven or whatever you call it, is everywhere. Here.

To see yourself as a thoroughgoing sinner is not a condemnation so much as a blessing, mercy. It means the light has dawned and you have started to see yourself as responsible with all the others, for the upholding of the world. It means you know you have a lot of archery practice to do, and you are already being handed another arrow to learn to become what you are. The spirit of compassion abroad in the world and seen in Jesus, in Buddha, in Mohammed, and in many, many human beings who cannot give allegiance to any religion, is always waiting, a ready teacher, to aim us through this dark age (for it is dark) at the centre of the target.

Who, says neither 'I' nor 'mine' hits gold, wins peace.

More Sex

It was Big. No - not George Michael's willy but his picture. All over the front of the Radio Times it was. Even Delia was relegated to a one-liner at the bottom. George Michael was interviewed by Parkinson on

167

prime-time television. Fair took me by surprise it did. Being of senior age and therefore significantly dead in the eyes of any 15-25 year old, I hadn't really heard of said George before he flashed his genitals in a public toilet in the States in 1998.

It all sounded a bit sick, and being a sweet and charitable Christian soul I took an instant dislike to his mandarin beard and face when it appeared on the screen and in the press. Yet here he was looking rather better. As I listened to Parky talking him out, I found there was emerging a sensitive intelligent human being who loved and honoured his mum and dad, who had integrity and was quite humble about his gifts which had brought him mega-star status. And he sang beautifully. He was able eventually to laugh gently at himself, caught with his trousers down, shamed, humiliated as he undoubtedly was.

Disgusting? Sad? Well perhaps no more disgusting or sad than the sexual displays and fantasies that many of us flash onto the wide screen of our hidden imaginations, behind our very private closed doors. Thoughts, pictures, indulgences we will never show to anyone. Sex is big, - go on admit it, even if you have had to sweep it under your own domestic carpet. If you watch TV. or listen to the radio long enough these days you can have sex in every conceivable position and combination. Why even golden oldie sex is now openly on the menu, lush and plush, slow and easy. Yippee!

However one thing is clear. There is no such thing as sexy football no matter what football managers keep trying to tell us. The sole aim of football is to score; to win, over the other. It is harsh, aggressive, warlike; skilful and practised maybe but all to easily there is a lot of dirty play. The beautiful game? You must be joking. Also whilst sexual union could frequently be happily described as a bit of a scrum, it should be a far, far cry from the sort of brutal clashes that take place say on the rugby field (that other football). Often enough though it is not.

Imagine if whilst the sex-game was on one of the so-called partners suddenly snapped out a yellow card from under the pillow, or desperately wanted to red-card the other off the field altogether!

How about Jesus then as a sex-therapist? Jesus the good-sex guide? Whatever you may think of him he is the perfect role-model for sex. Blasphemy! Sacrilege!

Now before Mr.and Mrs.Hot-under-the-Collar scrat around looking for a pen to write to Someone Important - think on. Jesus, as we often see him on a crucifix, pinned out on the cross, naked, the epitome of self-sacrifice, points the way.

Sex is not just about being bound by the laws of duty and obedience through the bonds of marriage, not infrequently back-breaking and distorting bondage. Nor is it about having it off with whoever, or changing partners frequently so long as no one gets hurt (what a self-deceiving joke that is). We are in dangerous territory here, full of manipulations, subtle dominations and over-shadowing, and a whole range of self-justifications which often simply disguise the drive which is secretly whispering 'I'm going to get what I want out of this. Give me satisfaction'. Whatever you think of Jesus he did not die on a cross saying 'I'm doing this for what I can get out of it'.

George Michael had the courage to admit that he was caught in the act of self-exploitation, selfish desire; randy, opportunistic. Not the best. He had the grace, I repeat, the grace, to admit in public that it was a degrading mistake. That means he can begin again to seek and recover in his own way for him, the innocence of a true sexual relationship.

Sex, the sex act, the complete sexual relationship - of which the sex act is only the beginning or the brief exquisite summing up of the whole drama of partners being together through all the times of their life - sex is meant to be an act of complete self-surrender, the one to the other. It is then as its most beautiful - and passionate - 'I give myself to you completely for your sake'. Whatever our relationship with our partner, whoever it is, within or without marriage, this is the key to its fulfilment. It starts with sex and works out from there into every fibre of life. Complete generosity. Abandonment to the other. It is commitment without limits. It is something few of us are good at physically or in our hearts. It is not one striving to or insisting on staying on top in all circumstances, the other giving way. But mutual surrender. Or it is always exploitation.

<u>To fail or not to fail.......?</u>

JESUS - A FAILURE!

He was a failure. Well he was. He finished up a total mess. The whole Christian thing begins with a man everybody called a failure. They even jeered and spat as he died. Imagine you and your friends gathering round someone dying in a hospital bed and yelling *"You stupid git"*. Then for good measure you gob on him as you leave. That's what it was like - he was a washout.

He didn't want all the titles people give him today - Sovereign Lord, King of Kings, Wonderful Saviour - names that are really just religious jargon - and in his lifetime he certainly didn't win any of them.

He finished being the worst thing a Jew could possibly be - and he was a Jew - a curse on his own people, for they said a hanged man is accursed by God. The final humiliation was to be stripped naked. For a Jew to appear naked was the ultimate insult, the final markdown. To be (a) crucified and (b) naked was worse than being stoned to death. You were a nobody.

So you see you are in good company, for if you are honest with yourself you know you, also, are a failure. Of course we pretend not to be, we keep up a good act.   We do not display our nobodyness. We paint our houses, clean our cars, pretend that the sex is O.K. or that we are now beyond that sort of thing, say just the right things. The world says you have got to appear as a success, that's the name of the game. And if you don't measure up - you're dead meat. But it's the wrong game.

(Interlude - a dead meat story. In major cities in South America there are thousands and thousands and thousands of orphan children. They run wild, appear and disappear everywhere like human rats. They scavenge and steal, harassing respectable citizens. They are known as the street children. In Sao Paulo the police (though they deny it) arrange most days to kill a few, to keep the streets clean. The children are a living sign of a nation failing to share its wealth and care for its people and they can't bear it).

We go for results and get tickled pink if we win, especially if we come out on top. We don't like to think of ourselves as hypocrites, but we are. Jesus had a name for hypocrites – 'Painted sepulchres' he called them, all white-perfect on the outside but inside…. That's why they hanged him of course, they couldn't bear it.

And you know, don't you? We don't want others to see how naked we are underneath. We know how many times we have failed others and even more important how many times we have failed ourselves. But we keep covering it up and pretend it never happens. Why else do we blame other people and get so self-righteous? Just imagine what a changed place the world would be if there were no self-righteousness. (I'm all right and you're not).

It's the wrong game. Our failures are just as important as our successes. They deserve equal acknowledgement and welcome. We are made for failure just as much as for success. If we don't take risks (and risk failure) we never get off the starting block, never leave the titty-bottle. Failure is as much part of life as eating and sleeping and we fail many more times than we succeed. If we never fail we never arrive. The playwright Samuel Beckett had it right:- "Fail. Try again. Fail better".

Our failures are not the end of everything. In human terms they may be disastrous, the worst possible pain, and if our proud cocky ego will not accept it we simply turn everything into Disney world. Perpetual great escapes full of anxieties and depressions. But if our failures are faced in our hearts and lived through, they open a new way. Forgiveness, as ever, is the key.

Jesus is saying to every human soul on this earth – "Do not be afraid when it has to happen, of being crucified along with me. I know what it's like. Failure may be the last thing you want but it may be the best thing you can have".

For a Christian and anyone else who is hungry to know - Good Friday, the ultimate hell-hole, and Easter Day, unbelievable new life, go together. Life and death are full of impossible miracles.

<u>Eyeball to eyeball</u>

We were on holiday with friends sitting round a table talking about rows between men and women. Not only do they happen (oh! so you've noticed), they are the stuff of life and one of the most potent causes of destruction and division in the history of the universe. Rows can of course be creative in that they clear the air and you can see more easily what right decisions need to be made, but more often than not they are bad news. How many battles, wars, have been started, vicious deals and bargains struck because a man and a woman have fallen out, gone off in a huff or a violent brainstorm. The fate of nations has been changed.

Some people, of course, love a good row, love to take it out on a partner, particularly if they feel they've got a good chance of making the other cringe or whimper, although sometimes it's a way, though not a good way, of restoring physical contact – "I threw beer all over him". However for most good and faithful trenchermen and women who are trying to make the most of life, each row is a hard pass and a place they would rather not have got to.

We were talking not so much about why rows happen - so often something quite trivial sparks it off- but what happens when you get into it, what attitudes and postures men and women take, what's going on inside them and how you might resolve things differently. Or is it even possible? So here are some generalisations (that means not true for everybody) which seemed to chime in with the experience of some others.

In a row it seems that for many women it goes deeper straightaway than with a man; so indeed the world has come to an end! And they go silent and unresponsive and comprehensively lock out the other. It seems as if they shut off, become impenetrable in order not to be hurt further. Women stay silent, for hours, days, even a week or two. Some work hard at not letting the sun go down on their anger, resolving the dispute before or at bedtime, for others, this is just not possible. They need more time.

Some men are more quickly up and down. They can get out of it more readily, think more immediately rather than feel more intensively, and they carry on as if nothing has happened. For them it has blown over, it's gone, matterless, tomorrow is another day, and this can often appear to the woman as if they are shallow, don't really care, etc.etc.

In all this, 'forgive/sorry' might be difficult for both to use. One woman I know who has over the years grown to manage the row better and see how inconsequential it is to their larger ongoing life, said that her husband could rarely use these words. So at the end of the day she would simply say "apology accepted" and that brought hostilities to an end.

What happens quite often with the man is that if the woman's silence continues when they have been willing to carry on as if it hadn't happened, then they start to shut off as well. Become monosyllabic or minimalist in word and expression, particularly if their placatory advances are patently rejected at this point in time. "Let her get on with it then and I'll get on with my own life". The sadness contained in this is that sometimes people start to settle for less and doors become permanently shut.

"We were married for X years" some say, "and never had a wrong word". What about the frozen, wrong, unuttered thoughts? How did they ever get to know one another at all, because the plus side of a row is that it is a way of learning.

How to get through all this? Patience of course. Some of you may have read 'Men are from Mars, Women are from Venus' (John Gray. ISBN 0-7225-2840). It's helpful. It suggests, among other things that women do not need men to help them out of their emotional hole with fine words, logical explanations and maps of the road ahead together. No, women are more in touch with their bodies than men and need some gestures of affection, some emotional touch or appeal to help bring them out. Since men are more likely in their curmudgeonliness to retreat into their own cold inner cave (black hole) defending themselves with intellectual mutterings and mind games, their need is for some affirmation and

173

approval of who they are and what they do. Slight things on paper, but hard enough in the emotional criss-cross of a row.

Of course men have to be prepared to be rejected in their tactile approach to recall their woman back to normal life; their move may be construed as a 'touching up in order to get me into bed', and not a few men have a skewed notion that 'sex will make it all right'. Oh dear. Sex can help, it can release pent up tears and fears, but only and maybe eventually.

Why am I writing all this when I myself am not a very skilled captain trying to navigate a tiny ship across huge seas? Well, partly because it can help to know that what happens to us happens to others. Also because rows often seem to blow up on holidays. Face to face at last, with none of the pressures of daily life to take the steam off or hide behind. So many couples I know have at least one good holiday row. The things that can flip it are as important as: ice-cream down a clean tee-shirt when you have no access to a washer; errors in map-reading (a favourite); things that should have been packed; the children, how to manage them on a rainy day; being just plain wound down and tired................

So if you haven't read it and are looking for a thoughtful, not escapist, holiday read (another row, not being left alone to read the book you brought). 'Men are from Mars...' might be just the thing. We will always have to work at it though, but then that's part of growing up.

Grandpa and grandma had quarrelled and grandma was so angry she would not speak to her husband. The following day grandpa had forgotten all about the quarrel, but grandma continued to ignore him and still wouldn't speak. Nothing grandpa did seemed to succeed in pulling her out of her sullen silence. Finally he started rummaging in cupboards and drawers. After this had gone on for a few minutes, grandma could stand it no longer. "What on earth are you looking for?" she demanded angrily. "Praised be God, I've found it" said grandpa with a sly smile, "Your voice!"

INTERLUDE

I was regretting the past
And fearing the future
Suddenly my Lord was speaking:
'My name is I Am'. He paused.
I waited. He continued.
'When you live in the past,
with its mistakes and regrets,
It is hard. I am not there.
My name is not I Was.
When you live in the future,
With its problems and fears,
It is hard. I am not there.
My name is not I Will Be
When you live in this moment,
It is not hard. I am there.
My name is I Am.'

Proud

'Proud'. I'm not good at 'proud' either for myself or for use with others. It's usually too full of the ego-stuff, the 'look at me', the 'look at us'. However I realise I do have something to be proud of: I am a 'liberal Christian', and I belong to the Church of England/Anglican Church, and I'm proud of it. I am not afraid to be labelled weak, indifferent, wishy-washy, not knowing what I believe, all these verbal adornments often coming in the direction of 'liberals'. I hear people say of the Archbishop of Canterbury, Rowan Williams, that he is wishy-washy, doesn't give a strong lead, speak out for one way or another. I like him as a leader because he thinks before he speaks, quite rare these days inside and outside the Church. This is strong leadership, but we much prefer someone around who will tell us what to think, it saves so much trouble and discomfort rather than having to work at it for ourselves over and over again.

So what do I mean by 'liberal' Christian? Basically learning to be set free from intolerance; not to tolerate intolerance. This in no way means 'just live and let live, I won't bother you if you don't bother me'. It means disagreeing profoundly with other people (like I do with my bishop and his proclamations on floods, etc. and divine punishment, God wagging a divine finger) but never treating them with disrespect because they are different from me in how they think and live. It means seeking to include in when others would cast out people they think not worth bothering about - off with their heads, slam them in prison, send them back home! It means regarding no one as inferior, everyone as my equal.

You think this is wishy-washy? I wish to God it was. It's sheer hard work, everyday. I have great black seams of intolerance running through me like coal seams, and I am forever in combat with them. Usually, but not always, it feels worth it in the end. This I believe is the way to freedom which is the basic gift of whatever you call democracy; of faith; of life itself. (Egremont Today is a fine witness to this inclusiveness).

Freedom never means doing what you want regardless of others, it is rather – "a positive social vision of shared freedom.............. To be liberal is not just the least worst thing: it is the best thing. If we are religious believers, maybe we need to renew the idea that liberalism is a sacred good, a gift from God. For surely, for example, there is a divine worth in a system that defends the young woman forced into an arranged marriage, saving her from patriarchal tyranny. Ought we not to have pride in this?" (Theo Hobson)

And of course in the end I have to say I have learnt all this through my Christian faith and what my teachers in the good old Church of England with all its limitations, have helped me to see about Jesus, called 'the son of man': what men and women are truly meant to be like. His harshest words are for hypocrites, those who deliberately practice double standards, who play to the gallery of public opinion, or political/doctrinal correctness, in order to avoid having to think. But he never writes them off, always seeking to include them in. And weeps over them, though so often they do not welcome his tears.

Quotation :-

"How does one become wise?"

Response:- "By reading the book that is you. Not easy at all for every minute of the day brings out a new edition"

Now

I am getting smaller. I remember the day, in my 40's, when I realized that my father was smaller than me, he was actually shrinking, diminishing. I went to the doctor a little while ago and he asked me how tall I was. I trundled out "5ft. 11 and ¾ inches". He said "You're not. That's my height and you're smaller than me!"

It is fashionable to say that 70 is the new 50: in terms of health and general capability people are now at 70 what they once were at 50. Older and fitter. For some, but it is certainly not the case for many people I know, and not particularly for me. I cannot walk the high fells any more, or run or swim properly (so recently, it seems, I could swim a mile a week!) My breathing is shorter than I would like it to be. And as for my skin-tone (oh my deah!) The fact is I am wearing out.

I don't know how long all this is going to take, and there are days when I find myself resenting it hugely. (You know, the usual, why me? stuff). I do all I can to prevent my diminishments getting in the way and seek a way round them, act as if they are not there. And that's O.K. too. But I am discovering that the key to living my present life to the full is when to let go. Not give up but let go, there's a world of difference.

It is a sheer waste of life's moments to hold onto griefs and regrets or past triumphs and satisfactions, things that are passing; what I could once do, how I once was, even if some of my contemporary friends can still do these things. We have only the present, today, now, this moment. All this I know is much harder for people who have had life's raw deal, who have been victims of poverty, accident, violence, disease, sometimes all the time. Yet this truth remains the same. This day, this moment, is our only real possession. To squander it, sticking in the past or fearing the future, is to miss it all.

And those who have suffered many diminishments, often at a much younger age, are usually my best teachers: very ordinary, very special heroes. Peter was dying of a brain tumour, and people said, "How brave you are, what faith!" - to which he replied - "Not at all, I'm just doing what lots of ordinary people do all the time".

Live as if you are going to live forever and be ready to let it all go, if you have to, if it is necessary, now. Become unstuck, as the Buddhists say, detach yourself increasingly as time goes by, then you will discern much more readily and immediately, what to hold on to, what to let go. And gratitude helps, finding things to be thankful for everyday. Every moment. As I am writing this, the phone goes with the news that Colin, just retired, has dropped dead on the beach on a walk. Another, on holiday at 53. John Thaw at 60.   Count your happinesses, they may be more than you think. Some days you can only do it by gritting your teeth; it is a discipline, but it helps build up the store of gladness. Rejoice, in your own diminishments, in the achievements of others, and tell them so.

The thing is, that though I am diminishing in body, inside I feel as if I am growing larger, stronger and indeed younger. And some others I know are the same. All is not what it seems, even though as a friend said "getting older can be a bugger". The 90 year old was being helped, by a young teenager.   In her day, she had been a real social whirler. She stopped to say, "Don't take any notice of what you see my dear, inside I am still an 18 year old who dances till dawn". And how about this - I met a younger man recently who regularly visits his elderly father now in residential care. They take a taxi to some of dad's favourite local viewing points and then walk back down. Brilliant care of the elderly that.

This is how a doctor, on radio recently, described our condition "We are all suffering from a fatal sexually transmitted condition. Life!" It helps to look Death in the face, the final diminishment, the complete, inevitable letting go. Letting go of everything except the present moment is quietly to prepare: put death in the frame instead of trying to pretend that it is there for everyone else but not for you or trying irrationally to neglect the tell-tale signs of diminishment and perhaps living in envy. Regard Death as a friend. We have it with us all our life. Did you know that 70% of all people in this country believe in life after death? So most people look forward with hope in and through their diminishments.

Talk about diminishments and death. Invite it into your family circle of friends and lovers. Talk with hope, for it is only one of the thresholds of life. Beyond is something else, a mystery. Be rightly suspicious of those who try to tell you in detail about life beyond death (heaven!?) Simply seek to believe with the poet Walt Whitman:- "I swear I will never henceforth have to do with the faith that tells the best! I will have to do only with that faith that leaves the best untold".

True Brit, true grit

Can you be Muslim and British is really a very silly question. Can you be Christian and British is to ask the same silly question. Of course you can. Both, at the heart of their daily practical living, have the same core values which we say are essentially 'British' - equality before the law, respect for the other person, respect for another's religion, fair-mindedness, fairplay; and to be relaxed and open, offering friendship rather than closed and hostile and excluding.

It is important to repeat that these are basic to Muslim belief and practice just as they are to Christian belief and practice. They have been down the centuries; in many countries, Christians and Muslims (and Jews) have lived in harmony together.

But Christian and Muslim faith and practice also rise above the horizon of being British and British nationhood. There are more important things than that. I have American friends who are utterly ashamed, at this time, to be American because of how the nation is behaving abroad and because of the sort of Christian fundamentalism that is taught in the majority of churches at home. This is not a nation they want to belong to, it is not a definition of what, to them, it is to be American. And I have felt that shame too about being British. Sometimes when going abroad in the last twenty years I wanted to hide away, no flag on the car, no national pride. And I also feel that on some issues right now.

It is quite right for Muslims who want to be part of this nation to feel deep in the gut of their faithfulness that certain things are wrong in the way we live, behave, dress, speak. And to protest when they perceive that they are not being treated as equals. They are entitled. Wanting to fit everybody into a fit-all box size was what Hitler attempted to do. Many Christians, just the same, protest about these things.

Of course there are parts of Christianity I really do not like, they contradict absolutely my take on my faith. I received this posting on the website of an American church just a few days ago – 'God hates Fags (homosexuals). God Loves Everyone? The Greatest Lie Ever Told'. It makes me so angry I could cheerfully blow up that little religious church/place. Many Muslims face the same angers, the same despairs, when other Muslims misuse the Qur'an and teachings of Muhammad to justify glorifying suicide-bombers and the massacre of innocent citizens. Some Christians will go to extremes, some Muslims the same. Acting on my anger however does not make it right.

So being British and Christian or British and Muslim is not all that straightforward. When 'society' (oh yes there is such a thing as society!), is changing, as it is in Britain, conflicts are bound to arise. Conflict in itself is O.K. just as conflicts between say parents and adolescent children are fine, (though they may be disturbing), healthy, part of growing up, for parents as for children. But abusing children with violence, either physical or verbal, is not fine. We have to learn to deal with our anger, the limits to our tolerance, in other ways. Even verbal abuse, verbal violence is no way on at all, which is where in our British democracy, we now have to learn to grow up together. Part of being a true Muslim or Christian is to practice patience, kindness and goodness, generosity, standing up for what you believe with self-control (no head-hunting), without being too self-righteously serious: one of the great qualities is learning to laugh when the chips are down. These personal skills have to be learned. They are also part of what it is to be a true Brit. And to practice developing such human disciplines until they become part of the way we live, takes as any true Brit also knows, true grit.

Dung

S--T. As they say on T.V. – *"Some readers may find what follows disturbing"*, offensive even. I don't know whether to be sorry about that or not. Sometimes our sensibilities need a little quiet tremble or sometimes a gale-shaking, though this is probably only a Force 2 wind (let the reader understand). So I'll begin again. *S--T.* Not with an exclamation mark but as a biological fact.

St. Julian of Norwich is, perhaps, the humblest, sweetest and gentlest of English saints (around 1342-1413). One of the holy things she said was that we should seek to praise God at all times and in all places. She said that going to the toilet well was just as much an act worthy of great praise and thanksgiving to God as any other activity; if you can't thank God for that, then where actually do you start?

A group had gone away on a sort of camping retreat in wilderness territory to search together for inner meaning in their lives. One day the leader said he was taking them to a local shrine in a sacred place. It was a hole in the ground. It was the latrine. He pointed out that we all need reminding that we are part of the ecological cycle, the great sacred cycle of creation, beginnings and endings. We have become sanitised and very cut off from our soil roots.

Go into one of our forests or great woods. Pick up a handful of soil and look around at all the green and growing life the soil nourishes. Within each handful of woodland/forest loam live approximately five billion microscopic plants – almost as many plants as there are humans on the planet. There are also close to one million animals and 100 miles of tiny root hairs in just one handful. When buried in the soil our soil becomes food for many of these things. Growth, exit, death, decay, rebirth.

The word '*humility*' comes from the word '*humus*' which means dung (a more polite S word). Local allotment gardeners know a lot about the value of dung. Humus gets dug in, buried into the earth, disappears - but, without it, nothing is fertile for long.

Humility is about bowing low in reverence to every other human being; making way for them, acknowledging their presence and thinking of their interests before our own. Not thinking more highly of ourselves than we ought to think. We are not very good at seeing ourselves as dung so that others may grow and flourish while we remain hidden - even though in the life cycle our bodies are eventually quite likely to end up on somebody else's dinner table. Bowing low before others is what we are not very good at.

There is an old Jewish saying:- "*The reason no one can find God any more is that no one is willing to stoop so low*"

Tao, a Chinese view of the Wisdom of Heaven, says: "*Yield and overcome. Force is followed by loss of strength. The low is the foundation of the high.*" It is the same.

The Buddha says- "*Get rid, empty yourself, of all falsehood, this is the real dirt, in order to be filled.*" It is the same.

For Christians Jesus says: - "*Anyone who wants to be great among you must be your servant,*" and, "*unless you become as a little child (the smallest of the small) you cannot get into heaven.*" It is the same.

So you want to be happy

My heart breaks. Ah! how dramatic poor wee lamb. Who does he think he is, Hamlet? The thing is, my heart breaks all the time. And it breaks both ways. Today is the most exquisite West Cumbrian June day. The air is sweet. The sun is strong. Everything is green and budding and my heart breaks with its beauty. I'm speechless, I have no proper words for it. Then I turn to the newsprint in front of me and it is - rape, murder, arson, knifing, abuse, sudden death - you know the score. And my heart breaks again. I'm speechless. I have no proper words for it. Broken both ways. The oscillation between the extremes can be very fast, immediate; sometimes I feel I'm spinning in the middle of it all, like a weathervane in a great wind, first one way then the other. And hey! sometimes it's hard going. It is also equally very good. Am I just a crazy, mixed up rapidly ageing adult?

I must turn to the Wise Ones. They are there all down the ages. The atheist/humanist from Greek times on will say this is what it's like to be fully human. The religious/Christian will say this is what it's like to be filled with the Holy Spirit of God. This is how it is, is meant to be. They will both say, this is the engine of Creation fully at work within us. We are agents of Creation, part of the juice, the fuel of Creation. Makers of creation as we go, making it and being made. It is in our heads, our hands, in our DNA.

This oscillation, they will say, is the very stuff of happiness. There is no true happiness without somehow holding all this together, the only alternative is a running away into different escapes from the mass of Life. And to live fully each oscillation as it happens is exactly not to run away. Rejoice with those who rejoice, weep with those who weep. No kid! no let up. Neglect the one and you neglect the other, then the engine starts to falter, to run down.

They say, the Wise Ones, rejoice in the fabulous beauty of Earth and its places as you would rejoice in your tiniest newborn: or with that utter secret pleasure as you see the colours of those flowers, or the beetroot and leeks you planted, blessing you as they appear in your garden plot. Rejoice. And equally, accumulate the sorrows as you go, for they need you to reach them from the broken heart of your helplessness. You belong also with them and you can help those who have them to lift and carry, though they will never know you. We do not have to understand, or measure input and output, or utility value. Abandon all those things here. Only have faith in ourselves and our immense capacity for loving and giving, so little recognised, so very often held right back. Be generous. Pour your heart out every way up. It's the surest way to have your heart not only truly broken but truly mended.

Creation is with us. 'The Force is with us'. But are we with the Force? -ah, that is the question. I was once in a meeting of some 40 people when a little, middle-aged woman stood up in the midst weeping copiously. Everyone gradually fell silent. Eventually she looked around and said "How is it possible to feel so much joy and so much sadness all at the same time?!" She had discovered the secret of human life. The very gift itself.

A bishop, Irenaus, way back in the third century said "The glory of God is a human being fully alive".

Silent Witness

Oh no! not him again, he's been at it too long: responses ranging
from "When is he going to be a real Christian and be firm and clear
about God's Law and Jesus as the Risen Lord?" - and all that to –
"Why doesn't he say something that will HELP me, who so often
feel so out of it, way beyond the fringe, yet trying to get on with my
life, sometimes with courage, sometimes in fear and trembling?"
It's a desperately uncomfortable world, that's putting it mildly is it
not? After yet another suicide bombing the young woman said, "No
one, nowhere, is safe anymore".

I long to say something here for your comfort but what do I say?
How dare I even put pen to paper? It's like going to visit the family
of Anthony Walker, that young black lad murdered in Liverpool,
with an axe buried in his head, or to anyone in shocked grief. What
do you say? Nothing. There is no consolation except perhaps your
being there. The simple silence of your presence. After the wife of
C.S. Lewis (The Lion, The Witch and The Wardrobe, etc.) died
quickly very soon after their marriage he said, "I don't want
anybody to say anything, I just want them to be there". And my
friend, dear Johnny, who, when I was in a mess some years ago,
just turned up on the doorstep with the words, "I don't know what
to say but I just had to come". (I remember after all this time).

The being there, just being there, is so often supremely the best
thing that can be given though we are afraid of it and it can never
seem enough. Alert. Courteous. Gentle. Take the rage, the terrible
anger, the deathly wounds into ourselves. Absorb them, let them
soak into you - for their sakes, but also for your own sake as a real
human being. Silent witness. The flowers, oh yes the flowers. The
black aunt of Anthony Walker arrives to witness the murder spot
and place her own flowers there. She finds white people already
there, silently. She turns to them "Thank you" she says "I didn't
know you cared". And they, gently, quietly, applaud her.
Meanwhile hundreds gather in the city, silently. A vigil of protest,
of communal shame. A vigil of grief.

And the flower of your simple presence, being there, wherever 'there' happens to be, from time to time, whether near or far away; being 'there' as best you can in your heart and soul and imagination, if not in physical presence. The London bombs - we were 'there'. The day after, a hundred Iraqis died. In a single day. 'There' also.

Silent witness. Do not be afraid to be cut to the quick, to choke and feel the tears coming for those all across the world. Do not, I implore you, give up, do not turn aside from the next horror (which will come) though we ache to do just that, switch off. Reach out. Reach out to whoever, to wherever, in your sense of helplessness. You, though you may be invisible to them, are their best token of hope. We must trust that, trust the Invisible; it can help them to recover some faith in themselves, in living. Your flowers are your prayer. Your own explosions of grief are your prayer. Your signing a book of condolence, is your prayer. Your donation is your prayer: your stunned shock. Stay with it, it is the best hope, for us all. Remember the African greeting, one word "Ubuntu" – "I am because we are". Hold on to it, say it over and over, let it be a glimmer of light in dark places.

That's enough words.

Silence and Stillness - God comes disguised as our life

What is there left to say about God? Nothing really. All that needs continually to be said is what you can't say about God; where God is not to be found. Blind alleys. Wrong signposts. The biggest thing you cannot say is:-1 believe in the Christian God as opposed to say Hindu or Muslim ideas about God, or Confucianism, Buddhism or even atheism. God is not greater or lesser than other gods. No comparisons are possible at all because the Godspot God I keep mentioning is different. Cannot be measured in any way we know. Off the scale. Even the word 'different' is a wrong word. We cannot measure God by any comparison we choose to make.

The best way to describe it is that God comes to us disguised. God comes disguised - as our life. And what is really needed is to experience God in the heart of our life. Oh yes! direct experience is very possible. Many millions testify to it, it becomes their article of faith, their driving force. But they will not find it easy to describe it to you, if at all. It is so 'different'. There are no words. The experience may be dead ordinary but is experienced as if from elsewhere, within us yet beyond us at the same time. And it's gone (for most people) as soon as it comes -disguised as our life. 'God' made himself 'felt' as the poets say.

It comes as a surprise, unexpected, and we may be troubled or given a real boost by this for quite a time. "I have been all my life a bell and never knew it until the moment I was lifted and struck. The vision comes and goes, mostly goes, but I live for it". (Annie Dillard - writer, microbiologist). If we want such experience we have to prepare for it and the simplest way, as many of the wise down the ages have always said, is by having some silence and stillness as part of daily life. In very short supply these days. But coming to rest, becoming quiet and still to collect ourselves, is crucial to human survival. We need to do it.

I love this bible story. A man called Elijah gets a message from within himself to stand outside the cave where he is hiding, and wait for God. A terrifying wind blows but God is not in the wind. Then an earthquake, then a fire, God is not in these either. Then there is 'the voice of silence' (also translated as 'a sound of sheer silence') and he hears God.

But I like this very recent story even better. First thing one Monday morning the present Bishop of Reading had in front of him a tough school assembly of 700/800 adolescents. And caught up in the crazy, fast-lane pace of his own life, he hadn't prepared anything. Panic. He starts off by droning on in the same old way, then after a moment or two he just stopped dead.   Then he found himself saying:- "What we all need to do is to just stop, stop being so frantic all the time and be still and pay attention to what's going on inside us. And that's what I am, we're going to do, for exactly one minute". So he took a chair and sat still for exactly one minute. He didn't say or do anything. When he got up there was a huge (his word) burst of applause. For days after he was stopped by several parents whose children had told them about this priest and the silent assembly and what he had said. (He's written a book now called 'Do nothing and change your life').

The poet R.S.Thomas said in one of his poems that there were no prayers said, but stillness of the hearts' passions, that was praise enough.

Doing God (Godspot – September 2009)

I 'do God'. Well of course I do. I realise it is really unfashionable for most people these days to do God at all. God for them, it would appear, is folk-lore stuff, old hat, not in the real world, and there's a lot of sniggering and laughing and scoffing and coughing when you mention 'God'. You're a nutter. But doing God is nothing to be ashamed of and I want other people to 'do God' because I believe God is a good thing. I do God because for me God is an inner compass: by constant reference to 'God' I swing back to the true North of my life. Indeed I would say of all Life. That true North for me is the big L, Love.

Of course it all depends on what you mean by 'doing God'. So for me doing God means God is within. Utterly within. The God who is without is for now almost totally, discredited, just like the present power structures. And 'within' I find is hard work. It's where we all began though -our first sensations, feelings, imaginings, thoughts, they're all 'in' there springing from the spark of life. And our present Western civilisation does all it can to wrench us out and away from withinness, everything has to be 'out there'.

The Quakers are a faith community who do and say one or two simple things around 'within'. Note, simple does not mean easy. They talk about an inner light, a light to live by. Their best way to discover it and the way it can shine up into your life is by going below all the radar of spoken and sung worship, words, images. Which is why they meet week by week and sit mostly in stillness and silence for an hour. A silence which they know only too well is bursting with imperfections, personal and universal. Yet they rest together. "Wait in the light" they say. There is strength in just being together as they wait for their inner light to switch in, never clear about what will come along, what illumination from within - if any. Maybe a reminder, or something unknown, beautiful, disturbing, comforting, deep, new; some peace perhaps. What they discover is that being still together helps to keep the inner light stronger in the huff and puff of daily life. This 'within', this inner light increasingly stays on and their personal climate as a human being can be transformed. Quakers become not scared of the silence, of the within. They 'do God' without doing anything in that hour, and sometimes it takes a lot of courage just to be there - in silence - doing God.

If God was not within I wouldn't bother. I 'do God' because God is within. Don't look for God anywhere else. I've discovered three things about Love in the life I have been enabled to live. True love never lets me down - ever. True love never lets me off- ever. True love never lets me go - ever, and is the only thing that has ever made sense of it all, my life. Nothing else works. If that's a definition of God, that's fine. You can only discover true love by going within and listening to the voice of silence, there from your beginning. Oh yes, silence has a voice, your own authentic voice. If you care to stay long enough, you will not be disappointed. True love and God within, they are the same.

A conversation via the late Anthony de Mello (the Society of Jesus).

"How does one seek union with God?"

"The harder you seek, the more distance you create between Him and you".

"So what does one do about the distance?"

"Understand that it isn't there".

"Does that mean that God and I are one?"

"Not one. Not two".

"How is that possible?"

"The sun and its light, the ocean and the wave, the singer and his song - not one. Not two".